# Submerged Cultural
Resource Management

# The Plenum Series in Underwater Archaeology

Series Editor:
## J. Barto Arnold III
Institute of Nautical Archaeology
Texas A&M University
College Station, Texas

---

International Handbook of Underwater Archaeology
Edited by Carol V. Ruppé and Janet F. Barstad

Iron and Steamship Archaeology: Success and Failure on the SS *Xantho*
Michael McCarthy

The Life and Times of a Merchant Sailor: The Archaeology and History of the Norwegian Ship *Catharine*
Jason M. Burns

Maritime Archaeology: A Reader of Substantive and Theoretical Contributions
Edited by Lawrence E. Babits and Hans Van Tilburg

Material Culture and Consumer Society: Dependent Colonies in Colonial Australia
Mark Staniforth

The Material Culture of Steamboat Passengers: Archaeological Evidence from the Missouri River
Annalies Corbin

The Persistence of Sail in the Age of Steam: Underwater Archaeological Evidence from the Dry Tortugas
Donna J. Souza

Submerged Cultural Resource Management: Preserving and Interpreting Our Sunken Maritime Heritage
Edited by James D. Spirek and Della A. Scott-Ireton

---

A Continuation Order Plan is available for this series. A continuation order will bring delivery of each new volume immediately upon publication. Volumes are billed only upon actual shipment. For further information please contact the publisher.

# Submerged Cultural Resource Management

## Preserving and Interpreting Our Maritime Heritage

Edited by

**James D. Spirek**
South Carolina Institute of Archaeology and Anthropology
Columbia, South Carolina

and

**Della A. Scott-Ireton**
Florida Bureau of Archaeological Research
Tallahassee, Florida

Kluwer Academic/Plenum Publishers
New York • Boston • Dordrecht • London • Moscow

Library of Congress Cataloging-in-Publication Data

ISBN: HB: 0-306-47779-3
      PB: 0-306-47856-0

©2003 Kluwer Academic/Plenum Publishers, New York
233 Spring Street, New York, New York 10013

http://www.wkap.nl/

10 9 8 7 6 5 4 3 2 1

A C.I.P. record for this book is available from the Library of Congress

All rights reserved

No part of this book may be reproduced, stored in a retrieval system, or transmitted in any form or by any means, electronic, mechanical, photocopying, microfilming, recording, or otherwise, without written permission from the Publisher, with the exception of any material supplied specifically for the purpose of being entered and executed on a computer system, for exclusive use by the purchaser of the work.

Permissions for books published in Europe: *permissions@wkap.nl*
Permissions for books published in the United States of America: *permissions@wkap.com*

Printed in the United States of America

# CONTRIBUTORS

**Arthur B. Cohn**
Lake Champlain Maritime Museum, Vergennes, Vermont 05491

**John R. Halsey**
Michigan Department of State, Lansing, Michigan 48918-1847

**Todd Hannahs**
San Luis Obispo, California 93401

**Lynn Harris**
South Carolina Institute of Archaeology and Anthropology, Columbia, South Carolina 29208-0017

**Susan B.M. Langley**
Maryland Historical Trust, Crownsville, Maryland 21032

**Daniel La Roche**
Parks Canada, Hull, Québec, Canada K1A 0M5

**Richard W. Lawrence**
North Carolina Underwater Archaeology Unit, Kure Beach, North Carolina 28409

**Peter Lindquist**
Shipwreck Tours, Inc. Munising, Michigan 49862

**Cassandra Philippou**
Flinders University, Adelaide, South Australia, Australia 5001

**Philip Robertson**
Nautical Archaeology Society, Lochaline, Morvern, Argyll, United Kingdom PA34 5XT

**Della A. Scott-Ireton**
Florida Bureau of Archaeological Research, Tallahassee, Florida 32399-0250

## CONTRIBUTORS

**Roger C. Smith**
Florida Bureau of Archaeological Research, Tallahassee, Florida 32399-0250

**Tim Smith**
New South Wales Heritage Office, Parramatta, New South Wales, Australia 2124

**James D. Spirek**
South Carolina Institute of Archaeology and Anthropology, Columbia, South Carolina 29208-0017

**Mark Staniforth**
Flinders University, Adelaide, South Australia, Australia 5001

**Bruce G. Terrell**
National Oceanic and Atmospheric Administration, Silver Spring, Maryland 20910

**Gail A. Vander Stoep**
Michigan State University, East Lansing, Michigan 48824

**Kenneth J. Vrana**
Center for Maritime and Underwater Resource Management, Laingsburg, Michigan 48848

# FOREWORD

Writing to the governor of Florida in September of 1964, the president of the Florida Keys Underwater Guides Association expressed concern about proposed salvage operations on the shipwrecks of the Spanish fleet of 1733. The Guides went on record to ask the governor for help "to preserve these historical wrecks for the present and future enjoyment of the public." Subsequently, a similar request was sent to the governor by the Florida Upper Keys Chamber of Commerce, which wrote that "we feel strongly that the historic interest and attractions for our growing influx of skindivers produced by these wrecks is much more valuable to the State of Florida than the 25% share gained from salvage of these old wrecks and their treasures." Shortly thereafter, the Monroe County Advertising Commission wrote the governor that "the historic wrecks off our coasts are a part of our heritage to be enjoyed and seen and not to be despoiled. [Aside from] the discovery of occasional "pieces of eight" and/or artifacts by individuals or the hope of such discoveries, the underwater beauty of a wreck housing hundreds of fish or a mound of cannon balls is directly beneficial to our economy while concerted salvage operations would destroy permanently the lure of these wrecks."

But the notion that these underwater sites would best serve the public as historical and environmental attractions rather than to be picked apart under state supervision for personal trophies was an idea way ahead of its time. It would be twenty-five years before the state was persuaded to designate one of the 1733 shipwrecks as a public underwater park. In 1989, the wrecksite of *San Pedro* was officially dedicated amid much local fanfare as Florida's second Underwater Archaeological Preserve. Partners in the establishment of the preserve were the Keys Association of Dive Operators, the Islamorada Chamber of Commerce, and the Monroe County Tourist Development Council—the modern descendants of those organizations that had years earlier sought the state's assistance to preserve historic shipwrecks. The new preserve, enhanced by replicas of cannons long ago salvaged, interpreted by a bronze plaque, brochures, and underwater maps, was immediately adopted by the waterfront community as a valuable tourism resource. It later would also become part of the state park system and was incorporated into the Florida Keys National Marine Sanctuary shipwreck trail. As of this writing, there are seven underwater archaeological preserves in Florida, each of which is on the National Register of Historic Places.

In this book you will find similar stories of experiments with the public management of submerged cultural resources, from the early shipwreck trails in Australia, to historic watercraft on the bottoms of cold-water lakes, to inland waterway heritage corridors and offshore maritime landscapes. Reflecting the history, technology, and commerce of numerous cultures over several centuries, these sites include sailing and steam ships, barges and ferries, yachts and freighters, as well as warships and galleons that are interpreted for the visiting public. Established through partnerships between national or regional government managers and local waterfront constituencies, these underwater museums represent attractions that combine heritage, recreation, and ecology tourism extending historic preservation toward new horizons.

James Spirek and Della Scott-Ireton have compiled and edited what is to my knowledge the first published source describing the scope and breadth of today's underwater heritage trails and preserves. Each chapter reflects both the strengths and weaknesses of various strategies that have been attempted for the public interpretation and preservation of historic sites in aquatic environments. Not only will this book serve to document the progress of those strategies, but it will offer new directions for cultural resource management on future frontiers.

> ROGER C. SMITH
> State Underwater Archaeologist
> Florida Division of Historical Resources

# PREFACE

The following monograph is devoted to sharing some of the information presented at a symposium organized for the Society for Historical Archaeology's 33$^{rd}$ Conference on Historical and Underwater Archaeology held 4 to 9 January 2000 in Québec City, Québec, Canada. The symposium, entitled "Preserves, Parks, and Trails: Interpreting our Sunken Maritime Heritage," brought together fifteen graduate student, professional, and avocational archaeologists from the United States, Canada, and Australia to present their work and thoughts on improving public access to interpreted shipwrecks and other intertidal and submerged archaeological sites (Appendix A). The session discussant was Dr. Roger C. Smith, Florida's state underwater archaeologist, who provided a summation of the session's presentations. The symposium was organized by James D. Spirek, from the South Carolina Institute of Archaeology and Anthropology, and Della A. Scott-Ireton, from the Florida Bureau of Archaeological Research, who also are the editors of this work.

The concepts under discussion at the symposium, and in this book, are the ways in which submerged cultural resource managers, archaeologists, avocationals, and historic preservation-minded organizations have joined forces to encourage public access to interpreted underwater archaeological preserves, parks, and trails. The interpretation of these underwater or intertidal attractions typically seeks to inform the visitor about the cultural significance, structural elements, and environmental setting of the site using illustrative guides, brochures, and ancillary land-based exhibits. Important goals of this submerged cultural resource management concept are to foster in the visitor a sense of preservation through stewardship and to provide education through recreation. Economic benefits for the host community derived through historical, educational, and recreational tourism also are significant objectives. The session organizers felt that bringing together experts in this sphere of submerged cultural resource management would provide a useful forum for discussing issues specific to the concept, such as the effects of increased visitation to unique and fragile sites, goals of interpretation, sustainability of the resource, and accessibility to non-divers, among other concerns and topics. The session also was intended to function as a clearinghouse of information that would prove beneficial to those who practice and to those who were interested in implementing this concept in their region.

In preparing the symposium, the organizers, now editors, invited practitioners of the concept to participate in the session. Additionally, the editors simultaneously posted a brief description of the proposed symposium to the Internet discussion group SUB_ARCH, devoted to discussing topics relevant to underwater archaeology, to elicit information about any existing preserve, park, and trail programs that were not widely known. Many responses to our letters and Internet request were received from various countries including Scotland, South Africa, Australia, Canada, Israel, and the United States. Unfortunately, several potential participants were unable to attend the meeting for a variety of reasons, although information about the geographical implementation of the preserve/park/trail concept became evident through this correspondence. The concept to promote and provide interpreted public access to submerged cultural resources apparently is limited to the United States, Canada, Scotland, Israel, and Australia. Elsewhere, countries either are just beginning to undertake creating preserves, parks, and trails, or are not yet prepared to embark on this venture.

The followings chapters reflect the majority of papers presented at the SHA 2000 symposium. Additionally, three papers were contributed as the book was in preparation. The order of the presentations and of the book was devised to open with a discussion of the principles of interpretation and management involved with this concept and then to provide existing examples of preserves, parks, and trails. The symposium concluded with a summation by Dr. Smith; here he provides a Foreword. In preparing their papers and, later, chapters, the authors were asked to focus on legislation, economic benefits, interpretation methods, problems, successes, and future directions regarding their preserve, park, or trail programs. The chapters presented in this volume touch on all of these aspects, as well as on many others that relate to the principles and practices of this innovative submerged cultural resource management idea.

The intent of this book is to disseminate the knowledge gained at the symposium to a broader audience including those who may be interested in establishing a similar program in their region, those who want to learn more about the historic preservation of underwater archaeological sites in the world, and those who simply may like to visit one of these unique archaeological sites.

The editors wish to acknowledge and thank the authors of each chapter for their hard work, patience, and support throughout the process of producing this work. We also wish to express our appreciation to Kluwer Academic/Plenum Publishers for this opportunity, and especially to Teresa Krauss for her help and motivation. Of course, our families deserve our thanks for their understanding of the time and effort necessary to make this book come together.

# CONTENTS

Introduction — 1

## PART I: THEORY AND CONCEPT — 3

1. Underwater Parks Versus Preserves: Data or Access — 5
   *Todd Hannahs*

2. The Maritime Cultural Landscape of the Thunder Bay National Marine Sanctuary and Underwater Preserve — 17
   *Kenneth J. Vrana and Gail A. Vander Stoep*

3. A Review of Cultural Resource Management Experiences in Presenting Canada's Submerged Heritage — 29
   *Daniel La Roche*

## PART II: PRESERVES AND PARKS — 43

4. Historic Shipwreck Preserves in Maryland — 45
   *Susan B.M. Langley*

5. From National Tragedy to Cultural Treasure: The USS *Huron* Historic Shipwreck Preserve — 59
   *Richard W. Lawrence*

6. The Visitor Schemes on the Historic Shipwrecks of the *Swan* and HMS *Dartmouth*, Sound of Mull, Scotland (UK) — 71
   *Philip Robertson*

7. Lake Champlain's Underwater Historic Preserve Program: Reasonable Access to Appropriate Sites — 85
   *Arthur B. Cohn*

8. Florida's Underwater Archaeological Preserves — 95
   *Della A. Scott-Ireton*

9. Beneath Pictured Rocks — 107
   *John R. Halsey and Peter Lindquist*

## PART III: TRAILS  119

10. Shipwreck Trails: Public Ownership of a Unique Resource?  121
    *Tim Smith*

11. Maritime Heritage Trails in Australia: An Overview and Critique of the Interpretive Programs  135
    *Cassandra Philippou and Mark Staniforth*

12. Florida Keys National Marine Sanctuary Shipwreck Trail: A Model for Multiple-Use Resource Management  151
    *Bruce G. Terrell*

13. Maritime Heritage on Display: Underwater Examples from South Carolina  165
    *James Spirek and Lynn Harris*

**Conclusion**  177

**Appendix A**  179

**Index**  181

# Submerged Cultural
Resource Management

# INTRODUCTION

The purpose of this book is to bring together in one volume a comprehensive body of work regarding the creation of underwater archaeological preserves, parks, and trails throughout the world. The book relates the continuing progress made by agencies and institutions that have sponsored these kinds of projects for over twenty years, as well as by those just beginning to introduce the concept in their region. Themes discussed in this work include historic preservation, tourism, education, and recreation, to name a few. This volume should be considered a primer for underwater archaeologists, both professional and avocational, and submerged cultural resource managers who wish to embark on encouraging and enhancing public access to suitable underwater archaeological sites. Additionally, this compilation will be of relevance to anyone interested in this concept as a form of historic preservation and, as a sort of travel guide, to those intent on descending into the water to visit the relics or to those wishing to learn more about a region's maritime cultural legacy.

The book is divided into three parts. Part I presents theoretical and conceptual constructs to consider when creating an underwater archaeological preserve, park, or trail. Three chapters comprise this section, outlining the decision-making process necessary to balance the desire for public access with archaeological integrity, presenting a theoretical framework for interpreting submerged cultural resources to visitors, and reviewing one country's ambitious program. Parts II and III of the book focus on the practical applications of creating these kinds of underwater attractions. Topics include enabling legislation at the federal and state levels, forging partnerships with public and private entities, developing infrastructure to minimize risk to diver and resource, and interpreting sites for both land and underwater visitors. Part II, consisting of six chapters, is devoted to those preserves and parks centered on single sites or localized concentrations of sites. The four chapters of Part III are dedicated to sites that have been "linked" together to form trails. In addition to conveying the practical aspects of creating and promoting public access to underwater cultural resources, the authors candidly explore the performance of their programs and offer suggestions and guidance for future work.

The editors and authors hope that those organizations wishing to create an underwater archaeological preserve, park, or trail will use this work as a means to achieve their ends, and as a looking-glass to foresee the kinds of issues and concerns that may arise as they embark upon this voyage.

# PART I: THEORY AND CONCEPT

Part I suggests a theoretical framework for the creation of underwater archaeological preserves, parks, and trails. The concept of providing and encouraging public access to underwater cultural resources is explored and innovative techniques for accomplishing this goal are discussed. As a relatively new method of submerged cultural resource management, ideas for creating preserves, parks, and trails still are being developed and expanded.

Todd Hannahs states that the main purpose of archaeology is recovering information from archaeological sites, rather than promoting access to sites. However, underwater archaeologists have found themselves, by default, in this position as a strategy to manage the behavior of those who desire to experience the tangible remnants of history. The author provides a decision-making paradigm for submerged cultural resource managers to use in determining whether to create underwater archaeological preserves that are closed to the public, or underwater archaeological parks that are open to the public. The determination of which sites are open and closed to public access is based on the principles of archaeology, rather than on the desire to provide an opportunity to experience history, traditionally the purview of historic preservation. This leads Hannahs to call for historic preservationists to go beyond the water's edge and to assist in the preservation of submerged resources as a natural extension of that discipline's goal of preserving terrestrial structures and providing historical experiences for the public.

Ken Vrana and Gail Vander Stoep discuss the concept of maritime cultural landscape and provide definitions for specific terms used to construct the over-arching concept of landscape. This concept seeks to provide an interpretive method for conveying a sense of the cultural and environmental contexts of a particular area. In Michigan, the maritime cultural landscape concept has been used in several regions, and the authors focus on one underwater preserve as an example of the practical applications of this concept. The chapter concludes with a list of challenges and opportunities encountered when using this theoretical construct to interpret the past.

Daniel La Roche reviews and assesses the means by which Canadian federal and provincial submerged cultural resource managers present information about the archaeology and history of submerged historical resources to visitors. Avenues of approach include interpretation centers and direct access to submerged archaeological remains at several parks. The author, while noting the successes of these programs, also remarks on the need for more work on both the federal and provincial levels to provide better dissemination of knowledge to the visitor and suggests means for improving public access to Canada's submerged legacy.

CHAPTER 1

# UNDERWATER PARKS VERSUS PRESERVES: DATA OR ACCESS

Todd Hannahs[*]

## 1. THE PROBLEM: PARKS VERSUS PRESERVES

There is something incongruous in the very nature of this book. Here we find a number of archaeologists devoting their thoughts and energies to improving and facilitating public access to submerged cultural resources. On the face of it this is not just strange but even a bit perverse. It is not part of the archaeological discipline to provide the general public with more and better opportunities to access cultural resources, be they wet or dry. That is not to say that such access is never a proper management approach for submerged cultural resources. It is, however, not desirable from a purely archaeological perspective. Nor is it what archaeologists have been trained to do. If the best use of a resource is to be made through public access and not through an archaeological recovery of information, should archaeologists be taking the lead in managing these resources? If the value of a cultural resource resides in its archaeological potential, then increasing the stress on that resource by encouraging public visitation is a bad idea. If the value of a cultural resource is not primarily archaeological, why are archaeologists taking the lead role in management decisions concerning them?

A place where the public is encouraged to visit and experience a submerged cultural resource is not a preserve, reserve, nor a sanctuary. It is a park. The purpose of a park is to provide sustainable access to the general public. This is what occurs when submerged cultural resources are opened to the public. Regardless of the reasons for creating an underwater historical

_____
[*]Todd Hannahs, 1250 Sydney Street, San Luis Obispo, California 93401.

park, the result will be a sanctioned increase in stress on the resource due to visitation by the public.

## 2. THE ARCHAEOLOGICAL APPROACH: CURATION OF DATA

Traditionally, archaeologists have assessed, recorded, and, in an increasing number of cases, opened to the public submerged cultural resources. Archaeologists find themselves working at odds with their own discipline for a number of reasons. Because underwater archaeologists were the first group to interest themselves in submerged cultural resources as cultural resources rather than as objects for salvage, they were originally viewed as the logical choice to be curators of these resources (Muckelroy, 1980:185). They have the most knowledge concerning these sites and the special conditions that apply to them. They have also shaped much of the thinking about the design and purpose of underwater reserves, sanctuaries, and preserves. But unless they restrict rather than encourage access, these are not places of sanctuary, nor preserves, nor reserves. They are places where increased public visitation is facilitated and encouraged.

The primary reason archaeologists are so involved in the creation and management of underwater parks is that no one else has been willing to take responsibility for the curation and management of these cultural resources. When an archaeological investigation of a shipwreck is completed there is often a considerable amount of intact structural elements and even artifactual remains left *in situ*. Raising such materials may not be financially feasible or even desirable from a conservation standpoint. But if the site is left unprotected then it may well be stripped clean, damaged, or destroyed by avocational divers or commercial salvors (Halsey, 1996:28). Even on those occasions when the archaeological considerations have been addressed, there has rarely been anyone to whom archaeologists can turn over stewardship of these resources.

Worse still are those situations where sites have been discovered but not yet adequately recorded or analyzed. Consequently, it is the archaeological community that has largely, by default, taken the lead in the design, creation, and management of underwater parks, preserves, reserves, and sanctuaries. They do so in order to mitigate the effects of behavior they cannot prevent (Cohn et al., 1996:vi, 1; Peebles and Skinas, 1985:49; Smith, 1990:23-29). The goals of preserving archaeological sites intact and encouraging public access are not only not compatible, they are, in many ways, contradictory.

The steps that have traditionally shaped the process of creating an underwater historical park are outlined in Figure 1. The goal is to recover information. The creation of an underwater historical park is ultimately a

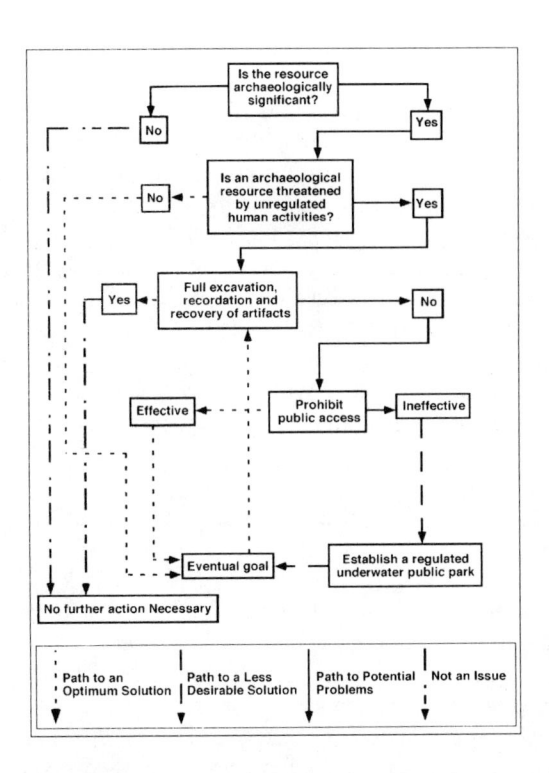

**Figure 1.** Current archaeological decision process for establishing an underwater park or preserve.

temporary measure that will ensure the preservation of the resource for future study. If all public access could be prohibited this would be a superior method to ensure the integrity of the site. Failing a complete prohibition on visitation, the creation of a park is the best of available alternatives. Consequently, much of the impetus for establishing underwater parks arises from a desire to protect and conserve these resources as much as possible, with the assumed goal that further archaeological investigation may take place at a later date.

Given that no other group has been willing to step forward and take responsibility for curating these resources, archaeologists have found themselves pursuing goals that are not archaeological. Given their training and approach to cultural resources, they are more inclined to regard cultural resources as data currently trapped in an historically deposited matrix than as a teachable moment or as a vital element in creating a shared sense of historical continuity (Cleere, 1989:9). While employing an archaeological mindset to manage underwater parks may be appropriate for short-term, site-specific goals, it is not the best model for treating a resource that one hopes will be available in perpetuity.

There are a number of benefits that can be derived from opening submerged cultural resources to the public. Many of them are addressed in this collection of essays: increased public awareness of the value and sensitivity of cultural resources; the economic benefits of heritage tourism; improved preservation where sites are under threat; a higher profile for underwater archaeological investigations; and a better perception on the part of the general public of the value of such investigations (Kaoru and Hoagland, 1994:194-197; Smith, 1998:115-119; Throsby, 1997:15-18). All of these are desirable goals. None of them, however, are archaeological goals. They may facilitate the achievement of archaeological goals by encouraging public support, but they do not, in and of themselves, further the basic purposes of archaeology.

## 3. THE HISTORIC PRESERVATION APPROACH: MANAGING ACCESS

So what is the proper mindset for managing an underwater park whose principle attraction is its historic component? First, a distinction between historic preservation and archaeology must be made. They are thought of by many as merely different elements of the same discipline. This is not the case, but the confusion is a common one (King et al., 1977:20-21). There is the old joke that describes the English and Americans as two people divided by a common language. This is something like the situation for archaeologists and historic preservationists. Both archaeologists and historic preservationists engage in cultural resource management. The vocabulary of both is rife with references to Section 106, legibility, integrity, and National Register potential. But archaeology seeks to retrieve information from cultural resources (Martin, 1981:18). When an archaeologist has finished his project, the physical remains are often found in marked zip-lock baggies, and the product is a report.

Historic preservation, on the other hand, seeks to ensure that the public can personally experience history (Fitch, 1982: 6-17). The goal of historic preservation is to maximize the number of opportunities available for society to come face to face with the physical remains of human activities. When an historic preservationist is finished with a project, he has a structure preserved *in situ* as his final product. Consider the following statement by historic preservationist Robert Stipe (1983:59):

> First, we seek to preserve because our historic resources are all that physically link us to our past. Some portion of that patrimony must be preserved if we are to recognize who we are, how we became so, and, most important, how we differ from others of our species. Archives and photographs and books are not sufficient to impart the warmth and life of a

> physical heritage. The shadow simply does not capture the essence of the object.

The shadow he is referring to is the essence and end product of an archaeological investigation.

Both archaeologists and historic preservationists value cultural resources. But the methods employed and the results sought are very different and at times may even be in conflict. Figure 2 presents the process from the standpoint of historic preservation. The focus is on providing sustainable public access, not on preserving archaeological data. One consequence of this is that physical intervention to preserve the resource is seen as an integral part of operating an historical park.

Currently, the creation and operation of historical underwater preserves strives to achieve two distinct goals. The information which resides in submerged cultural resources should be protected, and the resource should be available for the public to experience. When viewed from a solely archaeological perspective, the first purpose has been pursued by reluctantly allowing the second as an unfortunate but necessary side effect. Archaeologists open preserves to the public when the level of public access has already reached a point where the integrity of the data is imperiled (Peebles and Skinas, 1985:49). The chain of reasoning employed by archaeologists is laid out in Figure 1.

Ironically, it is often archaeological investigations which have raised public interest to an unacceptable pitch. This has resulted in the opening of sites which are particularly important to the archaeological community. Sites that are especially fragile, of exceptional antiquity, technologically unique, or especially rich in artifacts and contextual information attract the greatest archaeological interest. When the public learns of these sites, divers quickly seek to visit them on their own. The irony is that those sites archaeologists are most inclined to protect are often those which are under the greatest pressure to be opened to the public (Carter, 1997:A9; Green, 1997:A4).

When a shipwreck remains in context, as it does in an underwater historical park, archaeologists will continue to regard it as a site that will eventually require excavation and recordation. Improved technologies and techniques will allow new questions to be raised and, hopefully, answered. This has the result that an underwater historical park managed with an archaeological approach focuses on the protection of historic materials as a repository of archaeological information.

An historic preservation approach would focus on preserving the resource to encourage the public to experience their cultural heritage directly. Direct physical intervention to maintain the resource and to mitigate stress from

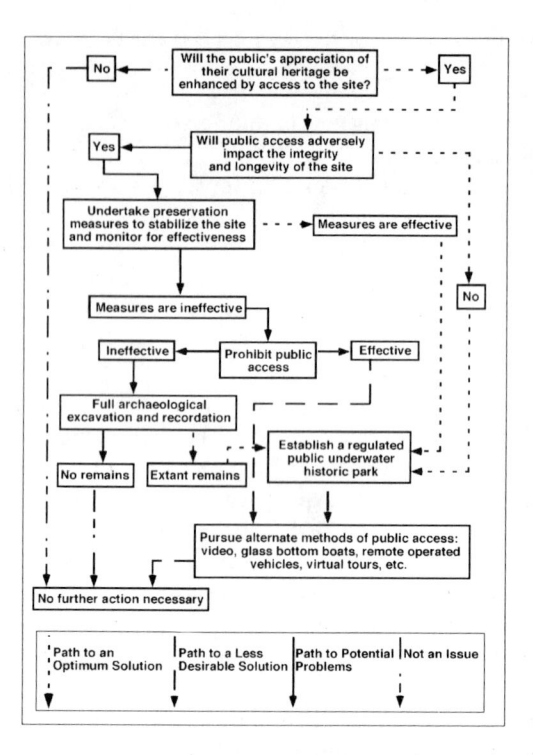

**Figure 2.** Historic preservation decision process for establishing an underwater historic park.

visitation would be the primary management strategy. This would also mean that a simple wooden barge swept free of artifacts but easily accessible and in clear water would be much more likely to receive attention than a more complex site with a set of prescriptive conditions and technical details of interest primarily to archaeologists.

A more effective approach to establishing underwater historical parks would be to consider the archaeological data contained in a potential underwater preserve as an undesirable trait. Table 1 is one possible method for evaluating a submerged cultural resource in order to determine if it is an appropriate subject for an underwater historical park. If the data were recovered then the category would be given a positive value. This would mitigate against, rather than for, choosing sites of high archaeological potential. If a site is not threatened, then the rationale for opening it to the public is one of outreach alone and archaeologists should not actively encourage the opening of such sites until the data has been adequately recovered. By keeping the purpose of underwater historical parks firmly in mind, the methods employed and the ultimate results will be greatly improved.

# UNDERWATER PARKS VERSUS PRESERVES

Figure 3 presents the steps involved in integrating both the archaeological and historic preservation approaches in order to create underwater historical parks as opposed to underwater archaeological preserves.

For historic preservationists, physical intervention in order to maintain the resource is an acceptable management option (Weeks and Grimmer, 1995:18-24, 62). Where preservation measures are inadequate and attempts to prohibit public access fail, an archaeological investigation should be considered. But the emphasis should be on seeking sites that have a high potential to make history tangible to the public and that have a low potential for data.

Focusing on the archaeological importance of a shipwreck may blind managers of these resources to potential solutions. An historic preservation approach would seek to treat the site as a resource to be visited and

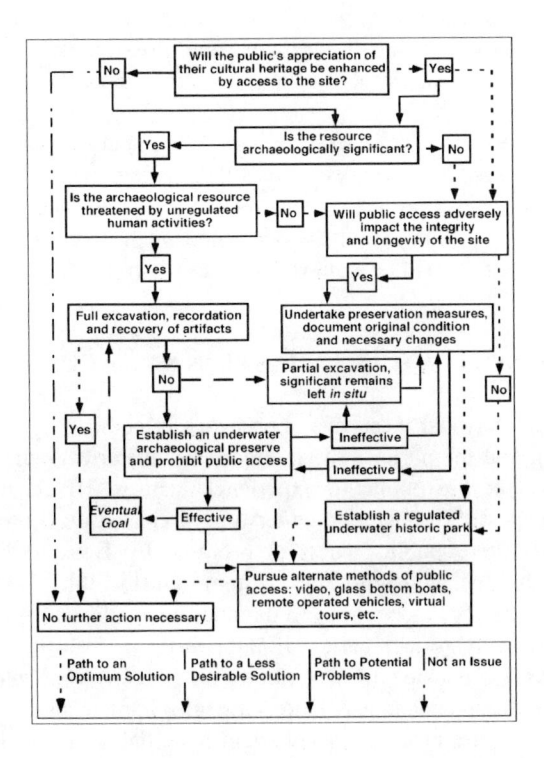

**Figure 3.** Optimum decision process for determining when to establish an underwater park or preserve.

experienced. This would place the treatment of the site on the same footing as other historic sites above water (Amer, 1998:20-24).

In the case of historic houses or historic ships, the treatment of physical stress resulting from public access and environmental conditions is a frequent issue for historic preservationists. The methodology and experience they would bring to underwater historical parks is more appropriate than a purely archaeological approach. In an historic house, or a ship tied up at a pier, physical maintenance rather than a host of prohibitions is the norm. With shipwrecks, all too often, such simple maintenance procedures are not even considered, let alone implemented.

The presence of data is a condition that can be ameliorated and the site then opened to the public. But archaeologists must acknowledge that there is a point where the best use of the site is to provide the public with a tangible part of their heritage rather than more information about that heritage. By seeing the data contained in shipwrecks as a negative aspect of an underwater historical park, these parks would no longer be asked to accomplish contradictory goals. Table 1 presents one possible way of evaluating submerged cultural resources for their potential to provide public access or information.

Since the question is whether to create a public park or not, the archaeological potential of the resource is largely negative. This allows clear separation between the protection and recovery of data and the creation of historical parks. By doing so at the beginning of the process, the likelihood that satisfactory results will be achieved is greatly increased.

## 4. SYNTHESIS: BALANCING CURATION AND ACCESS

A synthesis between these two approaches is possible. The first step is acknowledging that the purpose of an underwater historical park is to provide an opportunity for the public to experience history. If an archaeological resource needs protection, then an underwater archaeological preserve should be established where public access is prohibited. Besides the benefit of clarifying goals this will give the system considerable flexibility. An archaeological preserve can, when the data has been adequately recovered, be converted into an historical park. If necessary, an historical park that is suffering excessive damage from visitors can be converted into a preserve where it can be studied and conservation strategies implemented.

With less interest in the archaeological potential of a site, less sensitive sites can be considered as potential parks. Opening sites that appeal to the public, yet have little interest for archaeologists, will reduce the pressure on archaeologically sensitive sites by providing other outlets for the growing desire to dive on shipwrecks. For those sites that are too fragile or too dangerous to be opened to the public, alternate means of experiencing the site should be sought out. Various media have the potential of making shipwrecks accessible to a wider audience.

Table 1. Evaluation form for assessing potential underwater historic parks.

| Conditions | Quality of Historic experience | Archaeological significance | Vulnerability of resource | Safety |
|---|---|---|---|---|
| Current |  | N/A |  |  |
| Visibility |  | N/A |  |  |
| Depth |  | N/A |  |  |
| Temperature |  | N/A |  |  |
| Fauna |  | N/A |  |  |
| Traffic |  | N/A |  |  |
| Fragility |  |  |  |  |
| Historical Associations |  |  |  | N/A |
| Uniqueness |  |  | N/A | N/A |
| Loose Artifacts |  |  |  |  |
| Access |  |  |  | N/A |
| Representativeness |  |  | N/A | N/A |
| Integrity |  |  | N/A | N/A |
| Complexity |  |  |  | N/A |
| Modern debris |  |  |  |  |
| Totals |  |  |  |  |
| Final Value |  |  |  |  |

**Scale:**
5 = Outstanding
4 = Excellent
3 = Very Good
2 = Good
1 = Fair
0 = Neutral
-1 = Unfortunate
-2 = Undesirable
-3 = Bad
-4 = Very Bad
-5 = Disastrous

N/A=Not Applicable
*The presence of archaeological material would be valued -1 to -5

By viewing a shipwreck from an historic preservationist perspective, a more active conservation method is conceivable. That treatment would be sensitive to the legibility and integrity of the site. The concerns of archaeologists about the loss of data should be met by recording all repairs and rehabilitation work carried out on an underwater historical park and by making such work legible in both the archaeological and preservationist meaning of the word.

## 5. CONCLUSION

The underwater archaeological community has over the last thirty years created an entire sub-discipline from scratch. It has striven to change the public perception of submerged cultural resources and, considering the immense appeal of treasure hunting, considerable progress has been made. Archaeologists have developed new methods and new technologies for recovering information and for conserving recovered materials from submerged cultural resources. They have been active in seeking to educate the public about responsible practices concerning those resources. When it comes to underwater historical preserves, however, public access fundamentally conflicts with the goals pursued by archaeologists.

Archaeologists have stepped in to fill a need that has arisen because historic preservationists have not yet looked beyond the waters' edge. Just as a little over thirty years ago archaeologists struggled to move archaeology into the submarine environment, historic preservation has yet to "leave the shore." Archaeologists have been at the forefront of the creation of underwater preserves, but not because archaeology is fundamentally about providing public access to an authentic historic experience. They have come to it reluctantly. They are there because underwater preserves and parks are one way of protecting archaeological data. The failure of historic preservationists to take an active role in the design and management of underwater historical preserves has created a vacuum that archaeologists have had to fill by default. It is time for the historic preservation community to acknowledge its responsibility and to recognize that the discipline of historic preservation is a matter of methodology and philosophy, and not simply a set of certain structures in specific environments. That the public will benefit from this is clear. The historic preservation approach is well suited to designing and implementing underwater historical parks since its primary goal is to create opportunities for the public to personally experience history.

Underwater historical preserves would be more effective if they were divided into two distinct types: one labeled underwater historical parks which would be open to the public, and the other labeled underwater archaeological preserves which would be closed to the public. If and when the data has been recovered from an underwater archaeological preserve it could then be converted into an underwater historical park. The defining feature of an underwater historical park is its availability to the public. Its primary goal is to maximize that availability. Destruction or damage of the resource through excessive or inappropriate use would clearly curtail availability. Consequently, protection of the resource will certainly play a role in meeting the goal of availability, but protection is not the goal in and of itself. A clear distinction should be made between underwater archaeological preserves and underwater historical parks.

Archaeologists can assess a wreck for its information potential. If that potential is low, then recovering that information should require relatively little in the way of time and resources. The site can then be opened to the public as a park. Archaeologists should have only minimal further interest in the vessel. Once the data has been preserved the issues surrounding the establishment and maintenance of an underwater park become primarily physical. Is the site safe? What is the visibility? What is appropriate signage? How should the site be buoyed or otherwise marked? What legal protections and site monitoring will be necessary? What level of repair or rehabilitation is appropriate? What constitutes a valid historic experience for the diving public?

Once an underwater historical park is opened, the tools and philosophy of historic preservation are appropriate. The important issues are making history tangible to the public, integrity, legibility, preservation, and restoration. What is an appropriate level of intervention to preserve the resource? What constitutes a valid cultural heritage experience? When has integrity been lost due to alterations in the setting and feeling associated with the resource? These are the types of questions that concern historic preservationists.

The archaeological community possesses a wealth of technical expertise concerning shipwrecks. When establishing an archaeological preserve the archaeologists should have the final word. But in the case of underwater historical parks, it should be acknowledged that the primary goal is no longer archaeological.

The purpose of a park is to provide sustainable public access. Activities of restoration and physical intervention to sustain the resource should be viewed as being as normal and necessary as they are out of the water. Consider the amount of physical intervention employed over the years on USS *Constitution*, HMS *Victory*, or USS *Constellation* (Amer, 1998:20-24; Bayreuther, 1987:1-2; Roylance, 1996:8, 1997:25). Often, to make an historic site more accessible to the public, considerable intervention is seen as necessary and appropriate. These activities are clearly a key element in making maritime history tangible to the general public. In a park, where public access is allowed, the knowledge and expertise of archaeologists should serve the goals of historic preservation.

# REFERENCES

Amer, Christopher F., 1998, The South Carolina historic ships supply program, in: *Underwater Archaeology*, Lawrence E. Babits, Catherine Fach and Ryan Harris, eds., Society for Historical Archaeology, Atlanta, pp. 20-24.

Bayreuther III, William A., 1987, The USS *Constitution* Museum: telling the story of a national symbol, in: *Underwater Archaeology Proceedings From The Society For Historical Archaeology Conference*, Alan B. Albright, ed., Society for Historical Archaeology, Savannah, pp.2-3.

Carter, Elizabeth., 1997, Let technical divers explore shipwrecks, *Burlington Free Press*, September 23. p. A9.

Cleere, H. F., ed., 1989, Archaeological heritage management in the modern world, in: *One World Archaeology*, Volume 9, Unwin Hyman, Ltd., London.

Cohn, Arthur B., Cozzi, Joseph R., Crisman, Kevin J., and MacLaughlin, Scott A., 1996, *Underwater Preserve Feasibility Study of the Lake Champlain Canal Schooner O. J. Walker (VT-CH-594) Burlington, Chittenden County, Vermont*, Report to the Vermont Division for Historic Preservation, Montpelier, from the Lake Champlaim Maritime Museum, Ferrisburg.

Fitch, James Marston, 1982, *Historic Preservation: Curatorial Management of the Built World*, McGraw-Hill Book Company, New York.

Green, Susan, 1997, $100,000 set for study of sunken boat, *Burlington Free Press*, September 27, p. A4.

Halsey, John R.,1996, Shipwreck preservation in Michigan: Two decades on, *Common Ground, Archaeology and Ethnography in the Public Interest: Contested Waters* 1(3 & 4):27-33.

Kaoru, Yoshiaki and Hoagland, Porter, 1994, The value of historic shipwrecks: Conflicts and management, *Coastal Management* 22:194-205.

King, Thomas F., Hickman, Patricia Parker, and Berg, Gary, 1997, *Anthropology In Historic Preservation: Caring For Culture's Clutter*, in: *Studies In Archeology*, Stuart Struever ed., Academic Press/Harcourt Brace Jovanovich Publishers, Inc., New York.

Martin, Colin, ed., 1981, Protection of the underwater heritage, in: *Protection of the Cultural Heritage Technical Handbook for Museums and Monuments*, Vol. 4, UNESCO, Paris.

Muckelroy, Keith, ed., 1980, *Archaeology Under Water An Atlas of the World's Submerged Sites*, McGraw-Hill Book Co., New York.

Peebles, Giovanna, and Skinas, David, 1985, The management of Vermont's underwater resources: A model for shared responsibility, in: *Proceedings of the Sixteenth Conference on Underwater Archaeology*, Paul Forsythe Johnston ed., Society for Historical Archaeology, Boston, pp. 46-53.

Roylance, Frank D., 1997, *Constellation* goes dry, *Naval History* 11(2):25.

Roylance, Frank D., 1996, Home city to help the *Constellation*, *Naval History* 10(2):8.

Smith, Roger C., 1998, Discovery, development and interpretation of Florida's earliest shipwreck: A partnership in research and historic preservation., in: *Underwater Archaeology*, Lawrence E. Babits, Catherine Fach and Ryan Harris, eds., Society for Historical Archaeology, Atlanta , pp. 115-121.

Smith, Roger C., ed., 1990, Establishing An Underwater Archaeological Preserve in the Florida Keys, *Florida Archaeological Reports* 7, Tallahassee.

Stipe, Robert, 1983, Legal techniques in historic preservation, in: *Readings in Historic Preservation: Why? What? How?*, Norman Williams Jr., Edmund H. Kellogg, and Frank B. Gilbert, eds, Rutgers University, Center for Urban Policy, New Brunswick, pp.52 - 61.

Throsby, David, 1997, Seven questions in the economics of cultural heritage, in: *Economic Perspectives on Cultural Heritage*, Michael Hutter, and Ilde Rizzo, eds., St. Martin's Press, Inc., New York, pp.38-43.

Weeks, Kay D., and Grimmer, Anne E., *1995, The Secretary of the Interior's Standards for the Treatment of Historic Properties with Guidelines for Preserving, Rehabilitating, Restoring & Reconstructing Historic Buildings*, U. S. Department of the Interior, National Park Service, Washington, D. C.

# CHAPTER 2

# THE MARITIME CULTURAL LANDSCAPE OF THE THUNDER BAY NATIONAL MARINE SANCTUARY AND UNDERWATER PRESERVE

Kenneth J. Vrana and Gail A. Vander Stoep*

## 1. INTRODUCTION

The concept of *cultural landscape* appears promising as a framework for maritime research and resource management. The comprehensive nature of this conceptual framework, however, presents a number of challenges in practice. The purposes of this chapter are to discuss cultural landscapes in terms of maritime and coastal resources, and to explore the potential use of maritime cultural landscapes in Great Lakes protected areas. The paper is *not* intended to be an exhaustive treatment of the subject. Instead, the authors hope to spark interest and dialogue with archaeologists and cultural resource managers on its application in the discipline and field of parks, recreation, and tourism.

## 2. WHAT IS A CULTURAL LANDSCAPE?

Societies through time have affected and been affected by their physical, chemical, and biological environments to varying degrees. The cumulative effects of these interactions among humans and their environments are represented in contemporary landscapes. These landscapes include geographic areas with little human presence (e.g., wilderness), those dependent on extraction and use of

---

*Kenneth J. Vrana, Center for Maritime & Underwater Resource Management, P.O. Box 158, Laingsburg, Michigan 48848. Gail A. Vander Stoep, Department of Park, Recreation and Tourism Resources, Michigan State University, East Lansing, Michigan 48824.

natural resources (e.g., rural areas), and highly designed or built environments (i.e., suburban and urban areas).

*Cultural landscapes* can be viewed generally as settings created by humans over time that reveal important associations and relationships among people and the land or sea (NPS, 1997). A formal definition, developed in the United States by the National Park Service (NPS), describes a cultural landscape as "a geographic area, including both cultural and natural resources, and the wildlife or domestic animals therein, associated with a historic event, activity, or person or exhibiting other cultural or aesthetic values" (Birnbaum and Peters, 1996; NPS, 1992:107).

Four types of cultural landscapes identified by the National Park Service are historic sites, ethnographic landscapes, historic designed landscapes, and historic vernacular landscapes (Birnbaum and Peters, 1996; NPS, 1992). Historic sites

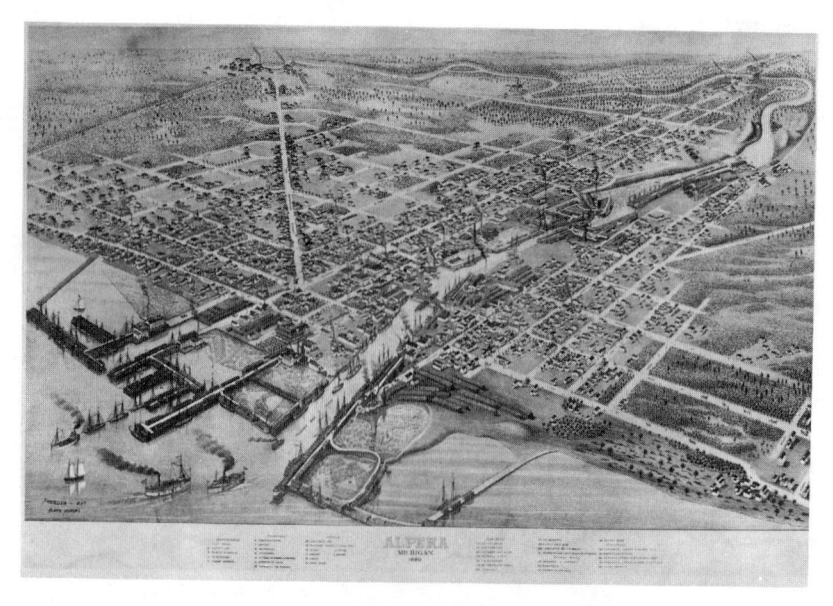

**Figure 1.** "Birds-eye" view of Alpena, Michigan (1880), a prosperous maritime center on Lake Huron

(photo courtesy the Jesse Besser Museum, Alpena, MI).
include buildings or structures usually interpreted within a more limited geographic context. Ethnographic landscapes are traditionally associated with a contemporary ethnic group. Historic designed landscapes have significance as a design or work of art relating to a recognized style or tradition.

*Historic vernacular landscapes* seem especially suited for interpretation of many maritime and coastal areas. They are defined by the National Park Service (1992:4) as:

> ...landscape[s] whose use, construction, or physical layout reflects endemic traditions, customs, beliefs, or values; in which the expression of cultural values, social behavior, and individual actions over time is manifested in the physical features and materials and their interrelationships, including patterns of spatial organization, land use, circulation, vegetation, structures, and objects; in which the physical, biological, and cultural features reflect the customs and everyday lives of people.

*Rural historic landscapes* are vernacular landscapes "that historically have been used by people, or shaped or modified by human activity, occupancy, or intervention, and that possess a significant concentration, linkage, or continuity of areas of land use, vegetation, buildings and structures, roads and waterways, and natural features" (NPS, 1992:4). Thematic types of rural historic landscapes, usually based upon historic occupation or land use, include agriculture, industry, maritime activities, recreation, transportation systems, migration trails, conservation, and religious or ceremonial activities (McClelland et al., 1990).

## 3. MARITIME AS CULTURE?

The term *maritime* commonly refers to relationships among humans and their water-based environments (e.g., oceans, lakes, streams, wetlands). Types of maritime activities include shipping, coastal trading, commercial fishing, water-based logging, boat building, coastal recreation and tourism, marine safety, and naval operations. Cultural resources associated with these maritime activities include ships and other large vessels; small craft; shipwrecks; shipyards; wharfs and docks; piers and warehouses; locks and canals; lighthouses, lifesaving stations, and other aids to navigation; coastal historic sites; naval facilities; and contemporary communities exhibiting a distinct maritime culture.

There continues to be some disagreement over what constitutes maritime *culture*. Muckelroy (1978) favored a more restrictive definition comprising all the aspects of ships and seafaring, but excluding related communities on shore and non-commercial activities such as coastal recreation. He presented the main elements of maritime culture under the headings of nautical technology, naval warfare and maritime trade, and shipboard societies.

Westerdahl (1994:265) advocates a more comprehensive list of activities that exhibit "a recurrent set of significant, maritime traits." The number of these behavioral traits, which serve as indicators of maritime culture, are extensive and vary by the particular society. A population must be "attuned to maritime preoccupations to be considered a maritime culture, even if the population resides at the sea shore. On the other hand, maritime culture follows the boat and its crew, even inland" (Westerdahl, 1999:1). Firth (1999) proposes that the *degree* to which a society is "maritime" can be analyzed in terms of four aspects termed locale, legitimized prerogatives, shared institutions, and inclusive identity. Research of maritime culture is proposed as "one of the ways to develop maritime archaeology from largely technological and naval aspects to a contribution to cultural history in general" (Westerdahl, 1994:269).

Hunter (1994) is skeptical about the analytic potential of maritime culture and the related concept of maritime cultural landscape. He suggests that, "although many cultures have maritime components, it would be difficult to find one which was entirely maritime other than in folklore...maritime components are no more than extensions or reflections of the broader culture to which they belong and are integral rather than isolated economic or social elements" (Hunter, 1994:262). He believes that these concepts were created primarily for political purposes rather than research, to help demonstrate that the "contexts of coastal and island sites are maritime as well as terrestrial" (Hunter, 1994:261).

## 4. MARITIME CULTURAL LANDSCAPES

Westerdahl (1992; 1994:266) acknowledges that "maritime cultural landscape was originally a term associated with the interests of cultural resource management...and was invented for the purpose of embracing all the present material remains at the shoreline, under or above water." He indicates, however, that the concept is worthy of scholarly research combining sea and land (Westerdahl, 1999). The cognitive aspects of cultural landscapes (e.g., intangibles such as tradition, folklore, and storytelling) should be considered in research as well as the archaeological aspects (Westerdahl, 1994).

Firth (1999) views the concept of landscape as one of three facets of maritime archaeology, including also society and critique. He believes that "the concept of maritime cultural landscape assists in identifying the relationship between the details of ancient maritime material and broader societal processes" (Firth, 1999:4). He proposes an expanded conceptual framework for research and resource management that includes maritime cultural landscapes, ancient land surfaces, the present situation, and the management environment (Firth, 1999). The present situation is defined as "the setting of everyday life at the coast here and now; the management environment means the physical and cognitive circumstances of the practice of managing archaeology." These broader, more contemporary conceptual frameworks indicate a need for applied research by a

# MARITIME CULTURAL LANDSCAPES

number of social disciplines, in addition to archaeology.

In the United States, the use of cultural landscapes as a conceptual framework for research and resource management is associated primarily with the National Park Service and the field of historic preservation. A cultural landscape report is the primary guide to treatment and use of a cultural landscape in the National Park Service (NPS, 1997). Ahern (1992:x) indicates that "early reports addressing landscape resources were single-discipline research projects which tended to concentrate almost exclusively on historical documentation." Subsequent reports include a review of archaeological records for the site, field survey data that documents the character-defining features of the landscape, analysis and evaluation of information from documentary sources and the field survey, and recommendations for preservation treatments (Ahern, 1992; NPS, 1997).

The process of analysis and evaluation focuses on significance, associations, and integrity (NPS, 1997). A cultural resource must have important historical, architectural, cultural, scientific, or technological associations to be significant. Associations are ties or relationships between a resource and its social-cultural context. A cultural resource has integrity if it retains material attributes representing these associations. Commonly accepted landscape treatments include preservation, rehabilitation, restoration, and reconstruction (NPS, 1997). The management of physical environments, wildlife, and other natural resources may be necessary in cultural landscapes as well as management of present-day human populations that use such landscapes for economic activities and recreation. Within protected areas, these landscape treatments and management strategies are usually described within a general management plan or equivalent, and other planning documents. In addition, the National Park Service encourages the nomination of significant cultural landscapes to the National Register of Historic Places as a site or historic district (NPS, 1997; McClelland et al., 1990).

The current National Park Service bibliography of cultural landscapes does not include any specific studies of maritime cultural landscapes. In Michigan, however, there are some on-going attempts to institute this concept within Great Lakes protected areas.

A regional approach to research and resource management was recommended for the Manitou Passage Underwater Preserve and adjacent Sleeping Bear Dunes National Lakeshore based on the concept of a maritime cultural landscape (Vrana, 1995). The Manitou Passage Underwater Preserve was designated in northern Lake Michigan by the State of Michigan in 1988. An inventory of its maritime and recreation resources was completed in 1995. The cultural landscape of the area is closely associated with the shipment of agricultural products and includes underwater resources (especially historic shipwrecks and dock sites), coastal historic sites, and "living" maritime communities now dependent primarily on coastal recreation and tourism. Sleeping Bear Dunes National Lakeshore plans to develop a cultural landscape study based on the themes of maritime and agriculture.

Statements of significance prepared for the Isle Royale National Park general management plan characterize this Lake Superior archipelago as a primitive wilderness and maritime park (NPS, 1998). Two distinct landscapes shaped these value-based images of park resources and perceptions of appropriate uses of those resources: a northwoods wilderness landscape and a maritime cultural landscape. The wilderness landscape is perceived as pristine woods and water dominated by wildlife and natural scenery. The extensive human history of Isle Royale includes copper mining by prehistoric people who shipped their cargoes by small craft over the open waters of Lake Superior, and many generations of fishing families of Native American and European descent. Other maritime themes of past and contemporary importance include coastal trading, shipping and shipwrecks, lighthouses, coastal resorts, recreational fishing, and pleasure boating. The challenge ahead is managing these two landscapes for preservation of wilderness experiences as well as present-day maritime recreation experiences.

## 5. THUNDER BAY NATIONAL MARINE SANCTUARY AND UNDERWATER PRESERVE

The Thunder Bay National Marine Sanctuary and Underwater Preserve, located in northern Lake Huron, provides a significant opportunity for applying a maritime cultural landscape as a conceptual framework for research and resource management. It is significant because of the quality of cultural resources and a commitment to federal/state/local partnerships.

The Thunder Bay Underwater Preserve in 1981 became the first shipwreck protected area established by the State of Michigan. In 2000, the National Oceanic and Atmospheric Administration (NOAA) designated an area of submerged lands and surface waters (including the underwater preserve) as a national marine sanctuary. The resulting Thunder Bay National Marine Sanctuary and Underwater Preserve is the first national marine sanctuary to focus solely on a large collection of historic shipwrecks and other underwater cultural resources, and the only sanctuary located entirely within state waters. The State of Michigan and NOAA jointly manage the sanctuary/preserve in coordination with local communities and other stakeholders (NOAA, 1999; Vrana and Schornack, 1999).

An informational foundation for the concept of a maritime cultural landscape was the *Preliminary Comparative and Theme Study of National Historic Landmark Potential for Thunder Bay, Michigan* (Martin, 1996). This study was completed as part of the feasibility process for designation of the Thunder Bay area as a national marine sanctuary. Theme studies analyze certain cultural resources and their association with particular topics or subjects in American history and culture. These resources are then compared with similar cultural resources located within a larger geographic region. The study by Martin (1996) indicated that the Thunder Bay area "contains a nationally significant collection of

# MARITIME CULTURAL LANDSCAPES

approximately 160 shipwrecks that spans over a century of Great Lakes shipping history.... Collectively, Thunder Bay's shipwrecks represent a 'microcosm' of the Great Lakes commercial shipping

**Figure 2.** Satellite photograph of Thunder Bay area, Michigan (1993).

industry as it developed over the last two hundred years" (NOAA, 1999:3).

Other studies produced as part of the feasibility process recognized that the Thunder Bay shipwrecks are part of a more extensive maritime cultural landscape associated with the themes of Native American inland shore fishery, water-based transportation, fur trade, European settlement, lighthouses and life-saving stations, commercial fisheries, water-based lumbering, shoreland mining, shipping and coastal trade, shipwreck salvage, coastal community development, and present-day maritime recreation. This landscape was described as the sanctuary setting in the *Environmental Impact Statement and Management Plan for the Thunder Bay National Marine Sanctuary* (NOAA, 1999).

The maritime cultural landscape will be an important conceptual framework in developing strategic management programs for the sanctuary/preserve, which will include resource protection, research, education, and recreation enhancement (NOAA, 1999; Vrana and Schornack, 1999). In particular, the collection of baseline information on this cultural landscape can assist in development of: 1) management strategies for underwater cultural resources within the sanctuary/preserve; 2) themes for public interpretation at museums and visitor centers in the region; 3) curricula for heritage education in local school districts; and 4) applied and integrated social/cultural research that includes present-day visitors and resident communities. This information can also assist in identification of historical and archaeological resources *not* located within the sanctuary/preserve that need protection and management.

## 6. CHALLENGES AND OPPORTUNITIES

As indicated or implied by this brief review of literature and practice, a number of challenges and opportunities exist in implementing the concept of maritime cultural landscape in Great Lakes protected areas. These challenges and opportunities are listed in the following paragraphs. Other issues involving the research and management of shipwrecks and other underwater cultural resources are summarized in *Technologies for Prehistoric and Historic Preservation* (U.S. Congress, 1986). The challenges of implementation include:

1. operationalizing the concept of maritime culture for rigorous social and cultural research;
2. coping with the comprehensive nature of cultural landscapes, including the collection and processing of large amounts of data and information;
3. developing multi-disciplinary and interdisciplinary approaches to inventory, assessment, and management of maritime cultural landscapes;
4. defining the boundaries of maritime cultural landscapes for practical applications in management that may not correspond with established political boundaries, or the perceptions of resident communities;
5. gaining public understanding and support for a complex conceptual

framework;
6. substantively involving local stakeholders in the design, planning, and implementation of maritime cultural landscapes to assure some degree of sustainability of these landscapes over time.

**Figure 3**. Exploring the side-wheel steamer *New Orleans* (wrecked in 1849) in the Thunder Bay National Marine Sanctuary and Underwater Preserve (CMURM photo by K. Vrana).

**Figure 4.** Archaeological survey of the historic shipwreck *New Orleans* in the Thunder Bay National Marine Sanctuary and Underwater Preserve (CMURM photo by K. Vrana).

Despite these challenges, there is also the potential to realize significant benefits from such a concept. Opportunities provided by fully implementing maritime cultural landscapes for research and resource management include:
    1.  a more robust analysis of maritime culture that focuses on the

associations and relationships among various aspects of the living and nonliving resources;
2. integration of the cultural past with the needs of present communities to better protect, manage, and sustain the landscape for the future;
3. meaningful public interpretation of these associations and relationships within protected areas, museums, and visitor centers;
4. stronger foundations for private-public partnerships within a landscape area;
5. a geographic framework for analyzing social-cultural significance and making research-based decisions in allocating limited resources to research and resource management;
6. a more systematic basis for evaluating geographic areas with maritime and coastal resources for designation as protected areas and heritage areas;
7. a more systematic basis for evaluating the results of existing protected areas in protection and management of maritime cultural resources.

In addition, the concept of maritime cultural landscape provides an opportunity to integrate research and resource management with the seemingly equivalent concepts of ecosystem and ecosystem management that are increasingly advocated in the natural and social sciences. A commonly accepted definition of *ecosystem* is "a community of different species interacting with one another and with their nonliving environment of matter and energy" (Miller, 1998:97). Ecosystem management can be defined as "the integration of ecological, economic, and social principles to manage biological and physical systems in a manner that safeguards the ecological sustainability, natural diversity, and productivity of the landscape" (Wood, 1994:6).

The concepts of landscape and ecosystem hint at more holistic and integrated approaches to research and resource management that lie ahead. These concepts also provide areas of common ground where different disciplines and fields may collaborate to reinvent the practice of resource management. Such collaboration appears necessary to sustain our maritime cultures as well as the physical and biological manifestations of these cultures.

# REFERENCES

Ahern, Katherine, 1992, *Cultural Landscape Bibliography: An Annotated Bibliography on Resources in the National Park System*, National Park Service, Washington, D.C.

Birnbaum, Charles A., and Peters, Christine C., eds., 1996, *The Secretary of the Interior's Standards for the Treatment of Historic Properties with Guidelines for the Treatment of Historic Landscapes*, National Park Service, Washington, D.C.

Firth, Antony, 1999, *Three Facets of Maritime Archaeology: Society, Landscape and Critique*, Department of Archaeology, University of Southampton, United Kingdom (December 26, 1999);http://www.st-agnes.org/~dcrank/student/FIRTH.HTM.

Hunter, J.R, 1994, Maritime Culture: Notes from the land, *The International Journal of Nautical Archaeology* 23(4):261-264.

Martin, Jay C., 1996, *Preliminary Comparative and Theme Study of National Historic Landmark Potential for Thunder Bay, Michigan*, Great Lakes Visual/Research, Inc., Lansing, Michigan.

Miller, G. Tyler Jr., 1998, *Living in the Environment: Principles, Connections, and Solutions*, Wadsworth Publishing Company, New York.

Muckelroy, Keith, 1978, *Maritime Archaeology*. Cambridge University Press, United Kingdom.

National Oceanic and Atmospheric Administration (NOAA), 1999, *Final Environmental Impact Statement and Management Plan for the Thunder Bay National Marine Sanctuary*, NOAA, Silver Spring, Maryland.

National Park Service (NPS), 1998, *Final General Management NPS Plan and Environmental Impact Statement for Isle Royale National Park, Michigan*, NPS, Denver Service Center, Denver, Colorado.

National Park Service (NPS), 1997, *Cultural Resource Management Guideline #28*, NPS, Washington, D.C.

National Park Service (NPS), 1992, *Guidelines for the Treatment of Historic Landscapes (Draft)*, NPS, Washington, D.C.

McClelland, Linda F., Keller, J. Timothy, Keller, Genevieve, P., and Melnick, Robert Z., 1990, *National Register Bulletin #30: Guidelines for Evaluating and Documenting Rural Historic Landscapes*, National Park Service, Washington, D.C.

U.S. Congress, 1986, *Technologies for Prehistoric & Historic Preservation, OTA-E-319*, Office of Technology Assessment, Washington, D.C.

Vrana, Kenneth J., ed., 1995, *Inventory of Maritime and Recreation Resources of the Manitou Passage Underwater Preserve*, Center for Maritime & Underwater Resource Management, Michigan State University, East Lansing, Michigan.

Vrana, Kenneth J., and Schornack, Dennis L., 1999, *The Thunder Bay Underwater Park and National Shipwreck Sanctuary: A Business Plan*, Center for Maritime & Underwater Resource Management, Michigan State University, East Lansing, and the Office of the Governor, Lansing, Michigan.

Westerdahl, Christer, 1999, *The Maritime Cultural Landscape: On the Concept of the Traditional Zones of Transport Geography*, Institute of Archaeology and Ethnology, University of Copenhagen, Denmark (December 26, 1999); http://www.abc.se/~m10354/mar/publ/cult-land.htm.

Westerdahl, Christer, 1994, Maritime cultures and ship types: Brief comments on the significance of maritime archaeology, *The International Journal of Nautical Archaeology* 23(4):265-270.

Westerdahl, Christer, 1992, The maritime cultural landscape, *The International Journal of Nautical Archaeology* 21(1):5-14.

Wood, Christopher A., 1994, Ecosystem management: achieving the new land ethic. *Renewable Resources Journal* 12(1):6-13.

CHAPTER 3

# A REVIEW OF CULTURAL RESOURCE MANAGEMENT EXPERIENCES IN PRESENTING CANADA'S SUBMERGED HERITAGE

Daniel La Roche[*]

## 1. INTRODUCTION

In the past, Parks Canada archaeologists were not only preoccupied with opening submerged cultural resources sites for divers, but also in delivering a range of interpretive products to the non-diving community. Several programs related to direct public access are reviewed here. When combined with an overview of the difficulties faced in the day-to-day management of submerged cultural resources it becomes apparent that the Canadian experience has been positive in many regards. Still, there are challenges to be resolved.

A new century is certainly a good occasion to review the intricate situation of submerged cultural resource management and presentation in Canada, and to propose new ideas to stimulate the field of submerged cultural resources management. Several economic recessions over the past years have forced budget and human resource cuts within all levels of Canadian government. At the same time re-organization of the federal public sector occurred which has resulted in the creation of governmental agencies such as the Parks Canada Agency.

Our country has also been impacted by the absence of dedicated legislation to protect shipwrecks and submerged cultural resources. The problem resides in the difficulty of harmonizing federal, provincial, and territorial levels of jurisdiction without infringing on each level. The small number of specialists in the field of underwater archaeology has also had an

---

[*] Daniel La Roche, Parks Canada, Archaeological Services Branch, National Historic Sites, 25 Eddy Street, 6th Floor (25-6-W), Room 177, Hull, Québec, K1A OM5, Canada.

impact on the level of public awareness for submerged cultural resources in Canada. For example, Parks Canada maintains a small archaeology team of eight which has a mandate to survey, investigate, and monitor sites within the entire National Parks and Historic Sites system. On the other hand, of all the provinces, only Ontario has an archaeologist who manages submerged resources within this provincial jurisdiction. He also trains as well as advises avocational divers on their projects to protect submerged cultural resources.

Although Canada has many submerged cultural resources, very few sites and historic places have been made accessible and organized for direct public access considering the dimensions of the country. The way archaeological resources are dealt with in Canada currently makes the creation of submerged preserves, parks, and trails for underwater cultural resources, even in the National Parks System, difficult.

Nevertheless, there have been some successful undertakings and this chapter reviews the best examples to be found within the National Park and National Historic Sites System. It also notes successful experiments undertaken outside the Parks Canada system. Finally, it looks at possible improvements to better disseminate information to the public.

## 2. TRADITIONAL PUBLIC ACCESS TO SUBMERGED FINDS IN PARKS CANADA INTERPRETATION CENTERS

Traditionally, public access programs were developed through Parks interpretation centers. These centers have been the cornerstone for the dissemination of knowledge about archaeological sites on land and underwater; they are still very important in the system. For example, the large-scale salvage excavations of the French frigate *Machault*, the Basque whaler in Red Bay, and more recently the Phips vessel, have all yielded information and artifacts from their time. This information was used in the interpretation centers and/or contributed to museum exhibits. Public access to these submerged archaeological sites was not allowed during the excavation because of accessibility, visibility, and complexity constraints. They were also judged less attractive for *in situ* presentation although they offered great potential for research on structural remains and artifacts.

The resulting museum-type exhibits have proven useful in demystifying the role of the archaeologist and in providing related disciplines with large collections of unique artifacts that are not found in archaeological land sites. For example, the Basque whaler site at Red Bay revealed to the world the first complete example of a sixteenth-century *chalupa* (whale boat), which was possible to conserve, rebuild, and present in an exhibit. The same feature would never have been accessible, visible, and reconstructed *in situ* (Figure 1).

Figure 1. View of the *chalupa* in the interpretation center at Red Bay (photo by P. Waddell, ©Parks Canada, Ottawa).

It is obvious that the traditional presentation methods used for submerged archaeological artifacts and features will continue to be very important channels for the diffusion of knowledge and physical evidence of discoveries. With the reduction of human and monetary resources for archaeological excavation, conservation, and presentation, it is now time to put more emphasis on the presentation of *in situ* resources.

## 3. DIRECT PUBLIC ACCESS AT LOUISBOURG HARBOR

In 1961, the first protected submerged cultural zone was created in Louisbourg Harbor, Nova Scotia, under the authority of Transport Canada. At the time, no diving was allowed in the harbor and Parks Canada was acting as an archaeological consulting agency. The remains of eighteenth-century warships associated with the siege events that occurred during the wars between France and England were the targets of such protective measures.

The documentation of the period accounts for the loss of four large vessels, all of which have been found. These are the only known examples of shipwrecks representing the 64- and 74-gun class of French warships for the period in North America. Although the sequence of events leading to their loss indicates that three of the ships burned to the flotation line, the *in situ* remains of the ships demonstrated that many features were preserved over time. They offered great potential for the understanding of vessel construction as well as the material culture and shipboard life of the period. It was not until 1986 that thorough investigations were undertaken by Parks Canada underwater archaeologists (Stevens, 1994). After completing a survey and a documentation phase, Underwater Archaeology Services analyzed the management options. It suggested leaving the remains to be managed in the most sustainable manner in their natural environment (Grenier, 1994). One important factor in the decision was the creation of what was called an underwater museum with *in situ* remains. The idea was to offer a different experience in providing direct access to genuine or untouched archaeological resources (Figure 2). Controlled public access was then authorized in

**Figure 2.** Cannons on the site of the *Célèbre* (photo by D. Pagé, ©Parks Canada, Ottawa).

accordance with the Harbor Master of Transport Canada in 1987. A permit system was instituted and delivered to a limited number of dive tour operators. Guidelines were developed by Parks Canada which had to be agreed upon by any dive tour operator seeking a permit.

The management of these sites for nearly thirty years had, overall, positive effects on the sites themselves and, after their initial discoveries and later evaluation, they suffered very little from human intrusion and looting. The archaeological recordings have consisted of a side-scan harbor survey, two site plans (Figures 3 and 4), photo and video coverage, and *in situ* artifact inventories and site condition reports. Very limited sampling and salvage of fragile material occurred. Although the security of artifacts on different sites was the main preoccupation for Parks Canada authorities initially, it has now shifted to a more global management approach where security is only one factor. Since the harbor was not, and is still not, included in the nearby National Historic Site, it was difficult to insure protection of sites by Parks Canada wardens. In 1996, the sites were designated of national historic significance. Such designation, however, does not confer any degree of protection to the remains. At this time, and until inclusion into the Parks realm, responsible tour operators and are still the answer to the security problem. Sites have now been accessible for more than twelve years and are still in a good state of preservation. Although the pressure from divers seems negligible, a monitoring program is in place to verify natural decay and human interference.

**Figure 3.** Artistic rendition of the site of the *Célèbre* (drawing by C. Pillar, ©Parks Canada, Ottawa).

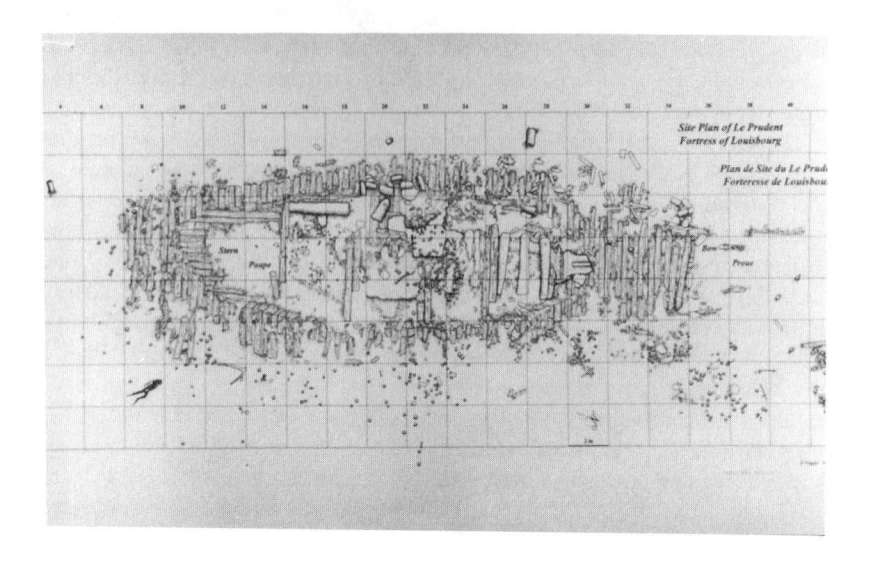

**Figure 4.** Site plan of *Le Prudent* (drawing by D. Larsen-Kapler, ©Parks Canada, Ottawa).

## 3.1. Description of the Public Access Program and Facilities in Louisbourg

Between 1987 and 1997, the site of the eighteenth-century warship *Célèbre* was the only site accessible for dive tours at Louisbourg and tour operators maintained accessibility to the remains by cutting the kelp covering the site. Any diver wishing to visit the site had to contact one of the permitted companies for a guide and boat services. The guidelines obliged the dive operators to instruct divers on the importance of protecting the resources and the rules to follow during the visit. The dive operators were also responsible for any damage to the sites. The tour operators eventually received the Nautical Archaeology Society (NAS) archaeological training to improve their awareness and knowledge of archaeology, but the information content of the tours remained their responsibility. Visitation peaked in the earlier years of opening but did not last long. Statistical records from 1995 to 1999 show that the overall number of divers accessing the sites has drastically decreased from one hundred thirty five to twenty seven. While 1999 was the first year where diving was permitted to all known sites (*Prudent, Entreprenant*, and *Capricieux*), no increase was noted.

An experimental promotional activity program by the firm Eco-Nova was tested in 1995 (Figure 5). Eco-Nova is a private eco-tourism company trying to develop learning experiences to be included in a vacation package for

**Figure 5.** Brochure advertising an international workshop on field techniques (courtesy Eco-Nova Corporation, Halifax).

European divers. The idea was to offer Part 2 (practical survey curriculum) of the NAS course on the *Célèbre* wreck in Louisbourg Harbor. Parks Canada agreed to provide recording grids and to supervise the work done by the students. Parks Canada also agreed to provide workshops on eighteenth-century material culture in its laboratory located at Louisbourg National Historic Site. Unfortunately, only one small group finally experienced the program and the project was soon abandoned.

Both the declining visitor statistics and the failed training attempt are indicative of the necessity to re-assess the management of these resources. The decreasing diver visitation to Louisbourg's submerged sites of national historic significance is certainly not due to the value or the state of preservation of the resources themselves, but rather to external factors. An analysis of past divers and the development of a diver profile would certainly help define what was, and is, the present diving public, and would help prepare new strategies.

Moreover, the harbor is still managed by the Transport Department and Parks Canada will eventually have to re-visit its role as co-manager of the resources. The sites also offer the potential for an integration of the shipwreck sites into the National Historic Sites family. This would definitely create national and international status, provide a proper level of protection, and ensure that adequate visitor services and programs are in place. Any new program would have to remain oriented toward the care and protection of the resources. In the meantime, it would be fruitful to put together an information package designed for dive tour operators and their visitors. In this way, the preservation message and the scientific and historic content of the guided tours would certainly be standardized, maximized, and balanced from one group to the other.

## 4. DIRECT PUBLIC ACCESS AT FATHOM FIVE NATIONAL MARINE PARK

In 1987, the Province of Ontario transferred Fathom Five Park to the National Parks System to become the first National Marine Park in Canada. The park was originally created by the province to protect a nice collection of popular shipwrecks endangered by looting divers. The park is now managed as a Marine Conservation Area (new terminology). The main preoccupation of the park is to protect the natural, self-regulating marine ecosystems which are important for the maintenance of biological diversity. The principles of protecting and conserving representative marine areas in Canada are embedded in a legislation which is in the process of being approved by the Government of Canada. Parks Canada's operational policy of managing any cultural resources found in these areas according to its Cultural Resources

Management Policy will remain in effect. This policy is instrumental in guiding the manner in which resources will be managed (Parks Canada, 1994).

Fathom Five includes twenty-seven shipwrecks encompassing most of the commercial types common on the upper Great Lakes during the last half of the nineteenth century. Most of the ships have been inventoried by Parks Canada archaeologists (Ringer and Folkes, 1991). Of these, thirteen are sailing vessels, including nine schooners and four unidentified vessels. There are also four steam vessels and four steam tugs which were engaged in the local commercial fishery. Seven other vessels have been only visited or have not yet been investigated. The shipwrecks lie in a wide variety of environments and depths, offering different learning experiences. Visibility is very good at most of the sites, but the light varies with depth. Historic shipwrecks are the most important and are practically the only submerged cultural resources identified in the conservation area. None of the shipwrecks have been considered of national historic significance. This means that all the resources have the same value and deserve the same level of care and protection. Since most diving is associated with shipwrecks, there is a monitoring program in place to assess both natural and human impacts on the resources (National Historic Sites Directorate, 1993).

There is no current accessibility restriction on the shipwreck sites, except for the *Sweepstake*. Accessibility to this small schooner is based on a timetable to allow visitation by divers and glass-bottom boats. This particular site caused special concerns to Parks Canada authorities because it was the most accessible and was visited by both divers and glass-bottom boats. The proximity to shore, the sheltered area, the shallow water, the high visibility, and the very good state of preservation of the hull were all responsible for its popularity. Unfortunately, this combination of natural and human factors began to alter the structure (Figure 6). The Park held public consultations in order to decide whether it was acceptable to intervene in order to regulate the visitation, to reinforce and stabilize the hull, and to prohibit entry into the vessel. The consultations helped define what the local businesses and dive groups preferred and what was acceptable within the Cultural Resources Management Policy. Most of the recommendations were accepted and the wreck remains accessible, but in a more controlled manner.

Any decision affecting submerged cultural resources in Fathom Five has a potential impact on seven to eight thousand people who make thirty thousand dives annually. In comparison, forty thousand people per year enjoy tour boat excursions. Divers, however, are the only visitor group who fully experiences the three-dimensional qualities of the aquatic environment. Diver registration has stabilized over the last few years even though quality services such as dive charters, air fills, equipment rentals, and emergency medical care remain available. The question now is which programs work and what can be improved.

**Figure 6.** View of the bow of the *Sweepstake* (photo by D. Pagé, ©Parks Canada, Ottawa).

## 4.1. Public Access Programs and Activities Related to Cultural Resources

Fathom Five currently offers:

- A small interpretation center operated by Parks Canada that provides basic information on the natural and cultural submerged resources.
- A fleet of glass bottom boats operated by private owners offering visits to several shallow wrecks.
- Sites accessible from shore for snorkeling which do not require Parks Canada registration.
- Scuba diving (partially controlled). This is the most common activity related to shipwreck visitation and means that a diver has to register at least once a year to be authorized to dive. When a diver registers and pays the fee, Parks Canada provides instruction on the basic accepted safety practices as well as on the ethics of caring for the

resources (the recommendations are simple: no anchoring on sites and avoid entry and touching of the resources).
- Mooring buoys to identify shipwreck sites.
- A leaflet with information on shipwrecks.
- A Web site where shipwreck sites are identified and briefly described:
http://parkscanada.pch.gc.ca/parks/ontario/fathom_five/english/dive_sites_e.htm

## 4.2. Opportunities for Improving and Developing New Activities in Fathom Five

Fathom Five, the oldest and the most frequented marine park in Canada for its submerged cultural resources, should lead experiments designed to increase its cultural content delivery to the public. Its 1998 Management Plan recognized a need to enhance interpretive opportunities provided to the divers. One proposal is to establish cooperative arrangements with other agencies to provide services.

The leveling-off of the number of divers is not alarming, but there is a need to redefine the interaction of Parks Canada with the divers visiting the historic shipwrecks. One possible approach would be to encourage divers to discover the characteristics of each historic shipwreck (technology, events, etc.). The development of questionnaires, for example, would help divers focus on something specific beside just the sporting challenge.

## 5. DIRECT PUBLIC ACCESS TO RESOURCES IN THE PROVINCES AND TERRITORIES

At the provincial and territorial level, archaeological legislation is instrumental in the management of submerged cultural resources, even though there are no submerged preserves or parks under these jurisdictions. A few registered and protected sites in some provinces (two in New Brunswick, two in British Columbia, and one in Québec) offer opportunities to develop divers' awareness and historical learning experience.

In spite of the limited legal mechanism and personnel (one full-time underwater archaeologist) in the provinces and territories, there is some work being done. Avocational groups, principally located in Ontario and British Columbia, raised the flag and tried to regulate their members and other divers. They have set up different activities on submerged cultural resources, mostly shipwrecks, often with the support of governmental authorities. Such activities as non-disturbing documentation phases on known sites, mooring programs on accessible sites, and surveys on large areas, have proven to be successful and have involved many divers across Canada. In Ontario, the group Save Ontario Shipwrecks published a series of brochures with the support of the province. It also maintains buoys in some popular and accessible dive sites in the province. These have been useful in raising public awareness of submerged cultural resources and have helped to nearly stop the looting of Ontario shipwrecks.

## 6. CONCLUSION

At this time, Parks Canada is still juggling with the educational potential offered by many important submerged cultural resources. Too little is known about submerged cultural resources and the few public access experiences tried to date. The reality is that Canada is a large country with a small population when scaled to the territory. It has a harsh climate, cold waters, and a short diving season. Many sites are in deep water and located in rural or remote areas.

Still, better public access in Canada can probably be achieved if some of the basic issues are resolved. These include:

- Creation of legislation to protect shipwrecks and submerged cultural resources at the federal level.
- Creation of submerged historic preservation programs, since natural reserves called National Marine Conservation Areas exist already.
- Establishment of more scuba diving rental services since the equipment is so costly.
- Increased budgets dedicated to cultural resources.
- Increased numbers of full-time professionals.
- Development of dedicated university programs in the field of submerged archaeology.

As these challenges are overcome, more direct public access facilities in accordance with Parks Canada cultural resource management policy will become possible. Joint venture management also offers new possibilities, as does a future open to emerging ideas on submerged heritage.

## REFERENCES

Grenier, R., 1994, The concept of the Louisbourg Underwater Museum, in: *The Northern Mariner/Le Marin du Nord* IV(2):3-10.

National Historic Sites Directorate, 1993, *Guidelines for the Management of Archaeological Resources in the Canadian Parks Service*, Parks Canada, Ottawa.

Parks Canada, 1994, *Parks Canada Guiding Principles and Operational Policies*, Minister of Supply and Services Canada, Ottawa.

Ringer, R. J., and Folkes, P., 1991, *A Marine Archaeological Survey of Fathom Five National Marine Park*, National Historic Parks and Sites Branch, Parks Service, Environment Canada, Ottawa.

Stevens, E. W., 1994, *Louisbourg Submerged Cultural Resources Survey*, Marine Archaeology Section, National Historic Parks and Sites Branch, Canadian Parks Service, Ottawa.

© Her Majesty the Queen in Right of Canada/Parks Canada 2002.

# PART II: PRESERVES AND PARKS

Part II focuses on underwater archaeological preserves and parks, highlighting a specific site or concentration of sites. These chapters present practical elements of creating underwater archaeological preserves or parks such as enabling legislation, developing partnerships, and producing interpretative materials. Of major importance are the pragmatic and varied experiences the authors describe in their efforts to create, maintain, and expand underwater archaeological preserve programs.

Susan Langley introduces Maryland's first shipwreck preserve on the remains of a World War II-era German submarine sunk in Chesapeake Bay. Langley follows with considerations and concerns for developing several potential preserves in Maryland's waters. While resource preservation is stressed, environmental conditions and legal implications in Maryland tend to discourage increasing public access to submerged cultural resources. Despite these limitations, state officials in cooperation with private interests are seeking to maximize accessibility to suitable sites on state bottomlands.

Richard Lawrence's chapter focuses on North Carolina's historic shipwreck preserve at the wreck of USS *Huron*. Wrecked in 1877 with significant loss of life, the ship has been reborn as a popular archaeological preserve. The author provides a history of the vessel and details the steps taken to create the preserve including providing access to sport divers and information for land-based visitors.

Philip Robertson addresses attempts by a local entrepreneur to work within the framework of Great Britain's shipwreck legislation to provide access to two shipwrecks in Scottish waters. After discussing the legal mechanisms used to manage shipwrecks in Great Britain, the author details the "visitor schemes" developed to promote sport diver access to the wrecks. Robertson shares the ways in which experience gained at these two sites can be utilized to expand access to suitable shipwrecks throughout British waters.

The underwater historic preserve program in Lake Champlain, Vermont, is presented by Art Cohn. This unique program seeks to balance the wishes of sport divers, who want to visit these well-preserved freshwater sites, and the desires of archaeologists, who yearn to record the sites while in a pristine state. This chapter details the practical components of creating Vermont's preserves and the continuing expansion of the program, as well as the subsequent management concerns surrounding public access to fragile sites.

The continuing evolution of Florida's underwater archaeological preserves is explored by Della Scott-Ireton. These preserves are located throughout the state and are the direct result of partnerships forged between state agencies and various entities in local communities. The Florida preserve system relies heavily on these partnerships to share in management responsibilities and to foster a sense of stewardship and pride in the individual community's submerged maritime heritage. The author recounts standardized methods developed through experience to create a preserve, along with necessary adjustments to reflect local conditions.

John Halsey and Peter Lindquist discuss Michigan's development of underwater archaeological preserves. The authors particularly describe the use of glass-bottom boats in an innovative program to provide public access to several shipwreck sites in Lake Superior. Developed as a business by a local entrepreneur, the glass-bottom vessels allow thousands of non-divers to view shipwrecks that previously only divers could visit.

CHAPTER 4

# HISTORIC SHIPWRECK PRESERVES IN MARYLAND

Susan B.M. Langley[*]

## 1. INTRODUCTION

At present Maryland has one historic shipwreck preserve with a second, Mallows Bay, in the acquisition and planning stages, and others are being considered at Historic St. Mary's City and Point Lookout (Figure 1). The first features a single resource, the German submarine U-1105; the second encompasses more than one hundred thirty wooden ships, most dating to World War I; and the others consider both maritime and once-terrestrial remains adjacent to Maryland's first formal settlement (founded in 1634) and an eroded Civil War prisoner of war camp and hospital at the mouth of the Potomac River. This chapter focuses largely on the extant preserve, its creation, and the general response to it, as well as problems encountered past and present, and possible solutions to these. Comparable discussion for the other planned preserves follows.

## 2. U-1105 HISTORIC SHIPWRECK PRESERVE

Late in World War II, when the tide appeared to turn against Germany and U-boat losses were catastrophic, fewer than ten submarines were fitted out with a rubber coating over their hulls and in interior hollows that might resonate (Pohuski and Shomette, 1994). This attempt to evade sonar

---

[*] Susan B.M. Langley, State Underwater Archaeologist, Maryland Historical Trust, 100 Community Place, Crownsville, Maryland 21032.

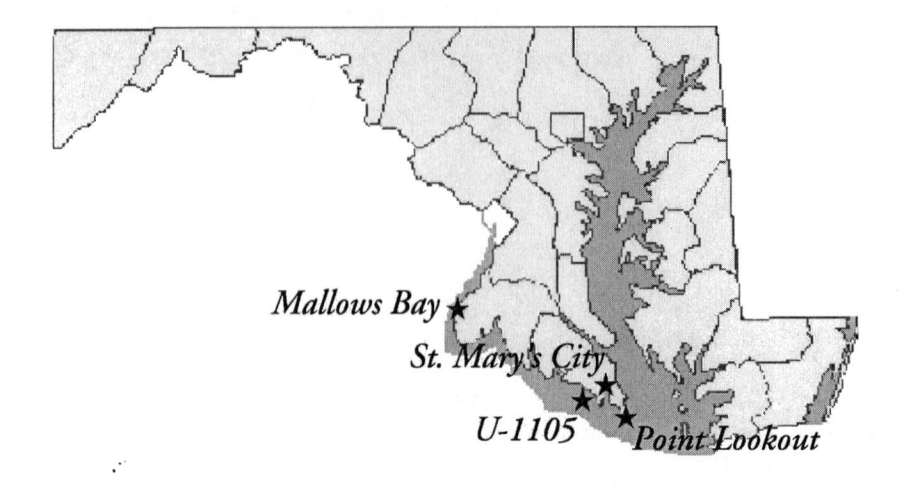

**Figure 1.** Map of Maryland with preserve locations (graphic by D. Curry, MHT).

detection and early effort at stealth technology, called the Alberich Process, had been known since 1939. While previously it had been deemed too expensive to undertake, by 1944 it was considered a worthwhile measure (Keatts and Farr, 1986; Stern, 1991). The U-1105 was one of these vessels and the only one known today.

Surrendered at the close of the War, it ended up in the United States for further study and, by the Cold War era, was being used for explosives and salvage testing. Sunk for the final time in September 1949 in the Potomac River off Piney Point, its location was lost through erroneous coordinates (Figure 2) (Pohuski and Shomette, 1994). The error was recognized and the U-1105 was relocated in 1985 by recreational divers. The sport divers kept the location secret until 1987 when it was revealed in a popular dive magazine (Keatts, 1992).

It was this disclosure that provided the impetus for the establishment of the preserve, aided by the fortunate convergence of a number of elements at all government levels and some private sector ones. Several members of the dive community were concerned for the safety and integrity of the site. They were very aware of the rapidity with which other submarine sites had been stripped and looted, such as the U-352 off North Carolina. They were equally

# HISTORIC SHIPWRECK PRESERVES IN MARYLAND

**Figure 2.** The U-1105 before, during, and after detonation of the test explosive, September 19, 1949 (photo courtesy Naval Historical Center, Washington, D.C.).

familiar with the recently passed Abandoned Shipwreck Act (P.L. 100-298, §1) and its Guidelines (55 FR 50116; December 4, 1990) that encourage states with maritime programs in place to create parks and preserves. Their familiarity stemmed from the fact that the Maryland Historical Trust (MHT) had just created the Maryland Maritime Archaeology Program within its Office of Archaeology and many of these individuals either had been directly involved in public meetings or were at least aware of the Program's existence (Annotated Code of Maryland Article 83B, §§5-601, 5-611.1, 5-620 and 5-630). A formal request for a preserve was made to J. Rodney Little, the State Historic Preservation Officer.

The U-1105 remains U.S. Navy property, although it rests on state bottomlands. Fortunately, the Navy has been the most active branch of the armed services in utilizing its share of the Department of Defense Legacy Resource Management Program monies to identify, document, preserve, and protect its resources. Recognizing the significance of the site and the severity of the threat to it, the Navy quickly partnered with the State of Maryland to assess the site and to fund the creation of the Preserve and the conservation of artifacts previously recovered by the sport divers who located the U-1105. In addition, the state developed a Memorandum of Agreement with adjacent St. Mary's County to aid in monitoring the site, to display and interpret the conserved artifacts, and to disseminate educational materials. Members of the dive community, originally individuals and a business (e.g. Michael Pohuski; Sea Colony Aqua Sports), and currently a non-profit organization, the Maritime Archaeological and Historical Society, aid in monitoring the site monthly when it is open (April-November) and deploy, retrieve, and maintain the mooring buoy each season, as per U.S. Coast Guard requirements.

None of the, perhaps, predictable problems were encountered in establishing the U-1105 preserve. This may have been partially owing to the alacrity with which it was undertaken, but is more likely due to the absence of jurisdictional questions. Navy title is undisputed and any theft, vandalism, or other offenses are felonies punishable under the Archaeological Resources Protection Act of 1979 (P.L. 96-96) and theft of government property laws which are more daunting than state legislation which considers such violations misdemeanors. Broad dissemination of the status of the vessel on brochures, web sites, and even on the mooring buoy appears also to be acting as a deterrent since only one instance of vandalism has occurred and that was within two to three months of opening the preserve on May 8, 1995.

A variety of methods to interpret the site were considered including guide ropes around the site and laminated maps. These were dismissed though, because the lines could potentially cause entanglements and the visibility is too low and the currents too strong to make the use of plasticized sheets either useful or practical. Nothing has been added to the site except a replacement closure for the main hatch which was removed by the discovering divers, and which is now on loan from the Navy to the Piney Point Lighthouse Museum. This closure is one-half-inch sheet steel and is not intended to replicate the hatch but only to prevent access to the submarine's interior and possible entrapment. The hull is in fact buried up to the conning tower and is completely full of sediment. Possible liability always plays a significant role in government undertakings but is of special concern in this situation.

The Maryland Office of the Attorney General (OAG) would probably have been much happier not to have a preserve open to the public at all. However, in light of the mandate to make submerged cultural resources available to the public, the OAG required only that the site be termed an "historic shipwreck preserve" and not a "dive preserve," to emphasize that the primary purpose is to protect the resource. The installation of a mooring buoy was likewise to prevent damage to the U-1105's hull structure and to identify Navy ownership. The buoy also bears text indicating that there are strong currents and poor visibility at the site. Partly because of these concerns and partly due to sheer logistics, the state does not provide any access to the site, which may be reached only by watercraft. Some dive shops, individuals, and charter captains in both Maryland and Virginia have taken visiting divers to the site or have organized special charters for specific training or for groups who arrange these, but only one shop did this with any regularity and it closed prior to 1998. Military and police divers use the site for specific training projects; about one such group per year visits the U-1105.

Approaches to site interpretation and heritage tourism are as varied as its audiences and beneficiaries. For the first two years of its existence, the site was interpreted through an exhibit at the Piney Point Lighthouse Museum and through brochures distributed by the Museum division of the St. Mary's County Department of Recreation and Parks, the U.S. Naval Historical Center, and the Maryland Historical Trust. In June of 1997, the St. Clement's Island-Potomac River Museum developed a traveling display and, that same year, the Maryland Historical Trust opened its web site: www.MarylandHistoricalTrust.net. The latter includes data about the U-1105 Preserve, providing interpretive materials and information on a global scale. This not only reduces inadvertent damage and general wear-and-tear on the resource but also makes it available to non-divers, families, armchair tourists, and researchers.

Efforts to monitor site use include requests to site users via the information on the buoy and in the brochure to "check-in" by radio or in person with either the St. Clement's Island-Potomac River Museum or the Piney Point Lighthouse Museum on arrival and upon departing the site. They are also asked to complete site use forms available from any of the federal, state, or county partners and also electronically on the MHT web site. In addition, the site is regularly monitored through direct observation by museum staff. The latter are trained to attempt to make radio contact with any vessels observed at the buoy that have not checked-in, prior to notifying the nearby U.S Coast Guard station to request an investigation.

Because of its relatively isolated location, the museum is a "destination" in tourism parlance; it is the end goal or sole purpose of a trip to the area. Much of the visitation to the museum is due to the tremendous popularity of lighthouses in general, but did increase with the inclusion of the U-1105 on the MHT web site. Certainly the museum's gift shop benefits, but it is difficult to measure any significant effect on other local businesses due solely to the establishment of the preserve. This is because these are so few (one gas station, two restaurants, and a couple of marinas) that they likely benefit from any visitation at all to the area. However, it must be noted that the site can be just as easily accessed by water from the Virginia shore of the Potomac River.

There is an additional level of complexity to interpreting and monitoring this site beyond physical logistics. The boundary between Virginia and Maryland runs along the mean high tide mark of the Potomac River on the Virginia shore, not down the center of the river as is often the case in other areas. Thus the submerged archaeological resources fall under Maryland's jurisdiction although they may abut Virginia. While this is not an issue with respect to the U-1105, management of other resources can require levels of cooperation and sensitivity that may be less prominent in other states.

Part of the reason more statistics are not available is that people do not fill out the site use forms which solicit a variety of data including numbers of visitors, as well as the gender, age, and interests breakdown of divers. The web site has provided a degree of information on interest based on site "hits" and requests for brochures and other information (Figure 3). This lack of feedback is the single biggest problem the preserve has experienced. Since the state does not control access to the site through a park entrance or other registration process, it is not possible to require the completion of this form or to gather statistical data by other means. The only method of attempting to regulate visitation is the seasonal removal of the buoy, which is not truly a deterrent to an insistent visitor with a boat and fathometer at his or her disposal. Additionally, limited winter hours at the museum makes visual monitoring less regular at this time.

This is not to say MHT does not hear from people. Members of the public call the office, send e-mail, and approach staff at archaeological and recreational dive sites to solicit information, to talk about their dives and general experiences, to seek permission to link their web sites to that of MHT, and so forth. Staff must then try to ferret out data from them: When did they visit? How many divers; ages; gender? Where did they stay; eat; fuel? Did

HISTORIC SHIPWRECK PRESERVES IN MARYLAND 51

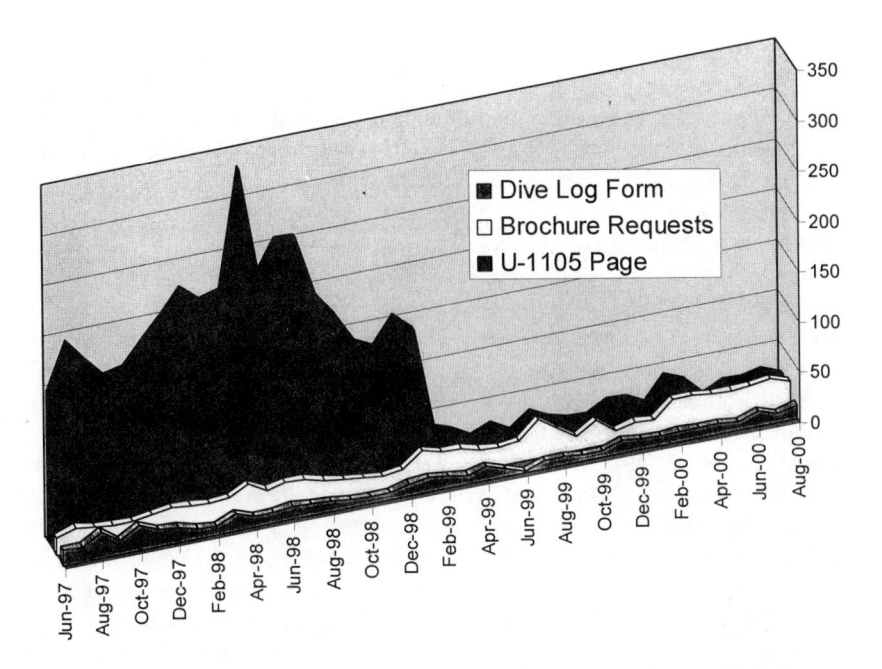

**Figure 3.** Graph of information requests, responses, and web site hits for U-1105 (D. Curry, MHT).

they come specifically to visit the site or was the visit incidental to other travel; business; etc.? Laziness is the chief reason given when asked why they failed to submit information, even on the electronic forms. A few individuals exhibit a general suspicion of any government agency asking for information, even when told these data are needed to justify funding for maintenance to keep the preserve functioning. Despite the lack of site use form submissions, the overall response to the preserve has been extremely positive.

The U-1105 Historic Shipwreck Preserve is a success. The primary goal of protecting the resource has been met, while still providing accessibility to the general public. The diving community may visit the site and everyone, including the non-diving public, may view historic and modern footage of the U-1105 both above water and sunken, as well as artifacts and models at the adjacent museum and via the Internet. Electronic interest ebbs and flows depending on which clubs or organizations have linked or severed links (usually the result of a server change) with the MHT web site, with current events in the media, recent lectures, and publications, or with the launching of submarine-related books or exhibits. Overall, interest is growing but obtaining useful feedback remains a prime concern.

## 3. MALLOWS BAY

A request for suggestions and comments from the public resulted in the current plans for the state's second historic shipwreck preserve farther up the Potomac River at Mallows Bay in adjacent Charles County. Mallows Bay is the repository for more than one hundred thirty wrecks, some of which may date as early as the Revolutionary War but most date to the early twentieth century in the form of World War I wooden steamships (Figure 4) (Shomette, 1996, 1998). Other vessels found their way into the bay during the Depression, such as the four-masted schooner *Ida S. Dow* which was brought from New England to serve as a dormitory for local salvage operations. Still others were abandoned there as a means of disposal with the reasoning that another vessel would hardly matter or even be noticed. The most recent of the watercraft are of World War II vintage. The shipwrecks of Mallows Bay provide a broad cross section of watercraft, both temporally and stylistically. Representative of this diversity are steam and sailing craft, a metal-hulled ferry (the last of its kind), a variety of fishing and work boats, and both merchant and military vessels as well as more mundane wooden barges. Many of these vessels protrude from the water and even more are exposed at low tide.

Although all of the wrecks are state-owned, as are the bottomlands, the creation of a preserve is not the clear-cut, relatively easy matter it might seem. With respect to the bay proper, the Maryland Historical Trust must coordinate with the Maryland Department of Natural Resources (DNR). The former is mandated to provide parks and preserves, but only the latter has the legislative authority to designate these areas. While this is not an insurmountable problem, it is one which requires consideration.

Another factor which has prolonged the planning process has been the acquisition of an adjacent land base. Until relatively recently, Mallows Bay was surrounded by privately owned lands. While this circumstance would not preclude the establishment of a preserve with only water access, it would also lead to people trespassing onto adjacent property for lavatory, picnicking, or photographic purposes. In addition, without a land base there is no way to monitor the site, either to prevent damage or to interpret the wrecks, or for

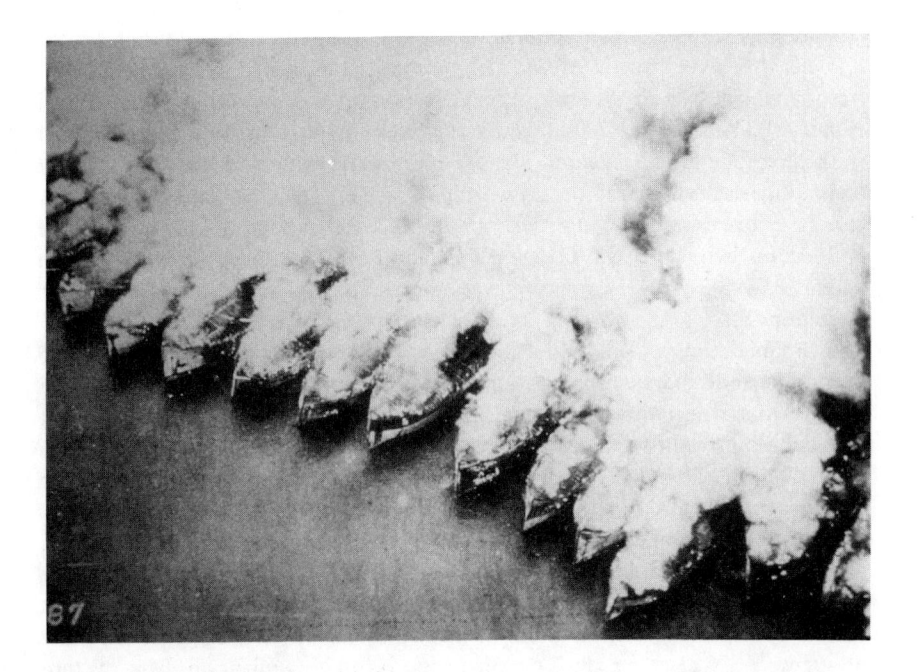

**Figure 4.** World War I wooden steamships afire in the Potomac River while awaiting disposal; many were later corralled in Mallows Bay (Frederick Tilp Collection, Calvert Marine Museum, Solomons, Maryland).

the safety of visitors. Since the site does not lend itself extensively to diving, being shallow, the formal creation of a preserve would tacitly encourage visitors to climb on the wrecks, leading to increased chances of damage to the resources and of injury to the visitors with no means available to summon emergency assistance or even to obtain rudimentary first aid.

Numbers of kayak and canoe tours are increasing annually as part of the current thrust toward heritage tourism activities, despite the nearest public launch and washroom facilities, as well as access to the river, being eight miles upstream on the Potomac River. Traveling against the relatively strong current makes a trip for hardy paddlers. The shallow nature of the bay leaves the wrecks exposed at low tide, making canoes and kayaks the logical craft to explore the site; spikes protruding from the hulls and other wreck components prohibit inflatable boats. Larger vessels are restricted to the single channel into Mallows Bay and cannot approach most of the historic vessels. However, other activities are possible, such as fishing and bird watching.

Beyond the historic character of the vessels in the water, there are a variety of sites on the surrounding lands (Native American, Civil War,

Depression). The preservation and interpretation of these sites make a compelling argument for acquisition of the properties in addition to the logistical reasons already provided. Further, situated at a main interface of fresh and salt water, natural resources abound and several threatened and endangered species thrive in the area. Charles County tourism and educational staff have identified several areas with terrific potential for low impact recreational activities and others worthy of varying levels of interpretation. A traveling display, extolling the possibilities of the site, was created in partnership with the St. Clement's Island-Potomac River Museum (from neighboring St. Mary's County) several years ago and remains in demand for popular events.

Organizations and individuals desirous of a preserve at Mallows Bay have been persistent and funding subsequently became available through a Clinton White House initiative (Fehr and Hsu, 2000:A15). The 5,500 acres that includes the Mallows Bay area is made up of four properties known collectively as Douglas Point. The owners range from absentee heirs to the enormous Potomac Electric Power Company (PEPCO). Negotiations for Douglas Point involved numerous federal, state, and county agencies as well as national and local organizations, private businesses, and individuals. These included the federal Bureau of Land Management (BLM) and the Department of Transportation through funding from the Transportation Enhancement Act program TEA-21, and the national non-profit organization The Nature Conservancy. At the state and county levels, the Maryland Department of Natural Resources' Open Space and Rural Legacy Program provided matching funds and worked with the Charles County Office of Tourism and Division of Parks and Grounds. The purchase moved cautiously, making considerable effort to ensure that the needs and concerns of diverse user groups are being equitably addressed, including those with competing interests such as a gravel quarrying company with a legitimate interest in the area. Final settlement on the properties is scheduled for 2002 (Jean Lipphard, personal communication, 2001), with the formal establishment of the preserve to follow shortly thereafter.

## 4. HISTORIC ST. MARY'S CITY AND POINT LOOKOUT

The two most recent candidates for becoming underwater preserves are areas adjacent to significant terrestrial historical sites: the cove beneath the corpus of the site of St. Mary's City, Maryland's first capital; and the waters around Point Lookout, site of Union Camp Hoffman for Confederate prisoners and Hammond Hospital, at the confluence of the Potomac River and the Chesapeake Bay (Mills, 1996; Leeson and Breckenridge, 1999). Both are in St. Mary's County and both suffer, to varying degrees, from erosion although Point Lookout has suffered most seriously, having lost two-thirds of the land on which the Civil War remains were situated. Anti-erosion measures either have already been undertaken or are in the process of being taken at both sites (Miller et al., 2001). Although erosion remains a concern, the creation of preserves at these sites relates more to potential damage from oyster dredging activities. As noted previously, MHT manages submerged cultural resources and DNR regulates oystering and has the capability of designating preserves. In this case both of the adjacent properties are not in private hands; Point Lookout is a DNR State Park and Historic St. Mary's City is a state-operated museum. Thus it would appear a much less complicated matter to create preserves at these sites than at Mallows Bay. However, something of a balancing act is still necessary. Created oyster beds in the cove at St. Mary's City bring commercial harvesters close to shore, well within areas that would have been part of the original historical land base. Closure of these beds would be perceived as interfering with a traditional lifeway of the Chesapeake Bay; as severely reduced as the oystering and crabbing industries have become, their iconic status makes them something of a "sacred cow" in this region. Although DNR actively creates oyster sanctuaries--planting spat and prohibiting harvesting of these beds--and is interested and willing to create such sanctuaries within the proposed preserves, two problems are faced. First is the aforementioned perceived interference with a traditional lifeway, and second, even sanctuary beds are periodically turned over with dredges.

In the case of Point Lookout, a proposed new sanctuary is on the Chesapeake Bay side of the Point close to the culturally sensitive areas (Figure 5). At this writing, DNR is coordinating an archaeological survey of the area in conjunction with MHT. At Historic St. Mary's City, one solution being considered is creating a new oyster bed for commercial harvest beyond the cove (a difference of less than thirty meters) and increasing its size as compensation for the cooperation of the local oystermen.

One, if not both, of these preserves will be established by 2003. As MHT and DNR gain experience in these cooperative endeavors, the process to establish preserves will become more streamlined and formalized and less based on a case by case approach.

**Figure 5.** The replica ship *Maryland Dove* moored in the cove adjacent to Historic St. Mary's City (photo by S. Langley, MHT).

## 5. CONCLUSION

On the whole, Maryland waters do not lend themselves to the establishment of dive parks in a traditional sense. There is a paucity of suitable sites, defined as sites that are sufficiently shallow, calm, and clear to permit safe visitation by the broadest spectrum of the diving and non-diving public while being of sufficient interest to draw their attention. Mallows Bay is probably the closest fit, although the diving visibility is poor. Near-zero visibility, the norm in both fresh and salt Maryland waters, frequently is coupled with strong currents; these factors generally prohibit on-site interpretation. Considering these severe strictures, underwater preserves are truly more for the preservation of the submerged cultural resources than for recreational diving. This does not, however, entirely preclude visiting or interpreting these sites. The Maryland Historical Trust is working with the National Park Service to locate and document sites related to both the Revolutionary War and the War of 1812, as well as to identify maritime resources off the Atlantic seaboard and in the interior bays of the barrier islands. With respect to the War of 1812, partnerships previously have been undertaken with the U.S. Navy and the Maryland Office of Tourism Development. MHT continues to seek out sites favorable to the creation of preserves, and advises and assists other agencies, educational institutions, and organizations seeking opportunities for interesting and educational diving experiences. Education and outreach play a significant role in Maryland's underwater archaeology program.

# REFERENCES

Abandoned Shipwreck Act, 1987, P.L. 100-298.
*Abandoned Shipwreck Act: Final Guidelines*, 1990, National Park Service, 55 FR 50116.
Archaeological Resources Protection Act, 1979, P.L. 96-96.
Fehr, S. C. and Hsu, S. S., 2000, Land, music museum slated for funds, *Washington Post* February 8:A15.
Keatts, H. C., 1992, The black panther U-boat discovered in the Potomac River, *Discover Diving* March-April:44-48.
Keatts, H. C. and Farr, G. C., 1986, *Dive Into History, Vol. 3: U-Boats*, Pisces Books, Houston.
Leeson, C. and Breckenridge, C., 1999, *Phase I Archaeological Survey of Point Lookout Tracking Station and Adjunct Theodolite Stations, Naval Air Station Patuxent River, St. Mary's County, Maryland*, report prepared for the Maryland Department of Natural Resources, NAS PAX, on file, Maryland Historical Trust, Crownsville, Maryland.
Miller, H. M., Mitchell, R. M., and Embrey, J. W., 2001, *A Phase One Archaeological Survey of the Beach and Nearshore Areas at St. Mary's City, St. Mary's County, Maryland*, report prepared for the U.S. Army Corps of Engineers, Baltimore District, Baltimore, on file, Maryland Historical Trust, Crownsville, Maryland.
Mills, E., 1996, *Chesapeake Bay in the Civil War*, Tidewater Publishers, Centreville, Maryland.
Pohuski, M. and Kiser, J., 1995, *Buoy Maintenance, Status Reports and Safety Guidelines on the U-1105 Black Panther Historic Shipwreck Pres*erve, report on file, Maryland Historical Trust, Crownsville, Maryland.
Pohuski, M. and Shomette, D., 1994, *The U-1105 Survey, A Report on the 1993 Archaeological Survey of 18ST636, A Second World War German Submarine in the Potomac River, Maryland*, report on file, Maryland Historical Trust, Crownsville, Maryland.
Shomette, D., 1996, *Ghost Fleet of Mallows Bay, and Other Tales of the Lost Chesapeake*, Tidewater Publishers, Centreville, Maryland.
Shomette, D., 1998, *The Shipwrecks of Mallows Bay, Inventory and Assessment*, report on file, Maryland Historical Trust, Crownsville, Maryland.
Stern, R. C., 1991, *Type VII U-boats*, Naval Institute Press, Annapolis, Maryland.
Submerged Archaeological Historic Property Act, 1988, Annotated Code of Maryland Article 83B, §§5-601, 5-611.1, 5-620 and 5-630.

**CHAPTER 5**

# FROM NATIONAL TRAGEDY TO CULTURAL TREASURE: THE USS *HURON* HISTORIC SHIPWRECK PRESERVE

Richard W. Lawrence[*]

## 1. INTRODUCTION AND HISTORICAL BACKGROUND

In the early morning hours of November 24, 1877, the USS *Huron* ran hard aground, sending a violent shockwave through the ship. The *Huron* had departed Hampton Roads, Virginia, the day before, embarking on a surveying expedition to map the coast of Cuba. Almost immediately after clearing Cape Henry and entering the open ocean, the *Huron* encountered heavy seas and gale force winds from the southeast. Near dusk the Currituck Lighthouse was spotted and the ship's captain, Commander George P. Ryan, ordered a course that would take the ship clear of Cape Hatteras and the treacherous Diamond Shoals. But something went wrong. Subsequent inquires blamed a compass error and a miscalculation of the ship's leeway as it battled the southeast gale. Whatever the reason, shortly after 1:00 a.m., the *Huron* struck bottom a short distance from the beach, near Nags Head, North Carolina. At first Commander Ryan thought his vessel had hit an obstruction, possibly a sunken shipwreck. But on seeing the tremendous waves breaking on the nearby beach he was heard to exclaim, "My God! How did we get here?!" These were among the captain's last words as he perished during the night along with ninety-seven other officers and crewmen (Figure 1). When the cold dawn finally arrived, only thirty-four men had made it safely ashore (Friday, 1988).

At the time of its loss, the *Huron* was a relatively new ship, having been built in 1875 at the Delaware River Shipbuilding Company in Chester,

---

[*] Richard W. Lawrence, North Carolina Underwater Archaeology Unit, P. O. Box 58, Kure Beach, North Carolina 28409

**Figure 1.** A contemporary drawing of survivors and victims on the beach at Nags Head with the wreck of the *Huron* in the background (*Frank Leslie's Illustrated Newspaper*, December 8, 1877).

Pennsylvania. Congress authorized the construction of the *Huron* and seven other vessels in an attempt to halt the unprecedented decline in American naval power that followed the conclusion of the Civil War. At the war's end the U.S. Navy was the strongest in the world with over seven hundred warships. By 1873, the Navy had only forty-eight obsolete vessels, and the United States ranked twelfth, behind Chile, as a world naval power (Coletta, 1987). Although solidly built, the *Huron* and its two sister-ships, *Alert* and *Ranger*, were transitional vessels between the old navy of the Civil War and the modern steel navy that began with the construction of protected steel cruisers in 1882. Known as *Alert*-class third-rate gunboats, *Huron*, *Alert*, and *Ranger* were the last U.S. Navy ships to be built of iron rather than steel and the last to have masts and sails to supplement their steam engines (Figure 2). The *Huron* measured 53.34 meters (175 feet) in length, 9.75 meters (32 feet) in breadth, and drew 3.96 meters (13 feet) of water amidships (Friday, 1988). Typical of a transitional period, the *Huron* was outfitted with a combination of antiquated and modern equipment. The vessel's ordnance and small arms consisted of Civil War-vintage cannon, single-shot pistols and rifles, and a fifty-caliber Gatling gun--a relatively new weapon for shipboard use in the 1870s. Likewise, in addition to its schooner-rigged sails, the *Huron* had a compound steam engine, a highly efficient design that had been in use on oceangoing ships for only two years when the gunboat was built (Friday and Lawrence, 1991).

The *Huron* served for two years with the North Atlantic Squadron, going to Mexico in 1876 to protect American interests during that country's revolution, and surveying the northern coast of South America and the Lesser Antilles islands in 1877. It was the vessel's sinking, however, and the accompanying loss of life that brought the ship national attention. Indeed, the magnitude of the disaster was compared to the loss of Custer's army, which occurred one year earlier. Tragically, when the *Huron* ran aground, the nearby Nags Head Lifesaving Station was closed, scheduled to open one week later on December 1 (Friday, 1988). Two months later, the steamship *Metropolis* ran aground twenty-three miles to the north with the loss of eighty-five lives, again demonstrating the inadequacies of the Lifesaving Service. Those two disasters prompted Congress to appropriate funding to build additional lifesaving stations along the North Carolina coast and to increase their months of operation (Means, 1987).

## 2. CURRENT CONDITION AND ARCHAEOLOGICAL INVESTIGATIONS

The USS *Huron* shipwreck site is located just two hundred and thirty meters from the beach at Nags Head in six meters of water. Since the mid-1970s, the *Huron* has been a popular dive site, particularly for scuba divers

**Figure 2.** The schooner-rigged *Huron* was among the last ships built for the U.S. Navy to be equipped with sails in addition to a steam engine (*Harper's Weekly*, December 8, 1877).

and snorkelers swimming out to the wreck from shore. In addition to its near-shore location, the *Huron* has the advantage of being located over twenty-six kilometers (sixteen miles) from the nearest inlet through the Outer Banks. This results in generally good visibility on the site since the murky waters of the sound do not influence the clearer ocean waters that surround the shipwreck. The amount of wreckage exposed above the bottom varies with the movement of sand in this dynamic near-shore environment. The vessel is aligned in an oblique angle towards shore with the bow only two and a half meters below the ocean surface. The stern shows damage from nineteenth-century salvage activities and is often level with, or buried by, the sand bottom. The remains of the *Huron* are covered by a thick layer of concretion and marine growth and serve as the home to abundant sea life (Figure 3).

One of the early and most frequent divers of the *Huron* site was Nathaniel H. "Sandy" Sanderson, at that time a Nags Head police officer. By the mid-1980s, Sanderson had taken the position of director of Nags Head Ocean Rescue. Among his staff of summer lifeguards was Joseph D. "Joe" Friday, a

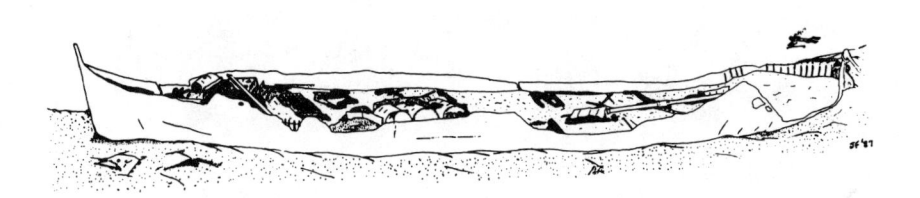

Figure 3. A perspective view of the *Huron* site (graphic by J. Friday).

graduate student in East Carolina University's Program in Maritime History and Underwater Research. In 1987, Sanderson and Friday applied for and received an underwater archaeological permit from the North Carolina Department of Cultural Resources to investigate the wreck of the *Huron*. Over the course of the next two summers, Sanderson, Friday, and their team of volunteer divers systematically mapped the shipwreck and produced an accurate site plan of the historic gunboat (Figure 4).

Although the project's main focus was to document the site, the group recorded and collected a number of artifacts that reflected the various functions of the ship: a home to one hundred and thirty-four officers and crewmen; an oceangoing steamship; and a naval fighting vessel. The artifacts included silver-plated eating utensils, ceramic plates, wine bottles with cork and contents intact, pipes, fittings, slate duty rosters from the engineering space, ammunition, bayonets, and a rare fifty-caliber Remington rolling-block pistol (Figure 5). The project served as the subject of Joe Friday's 1988 master's thesis that provided a detailed account of the *Huron*'s history and the ship's present condition. In 1991, Joe Friday and Richard Lawrence successfully nominated the *Huron* to the National Register of Historic Places.

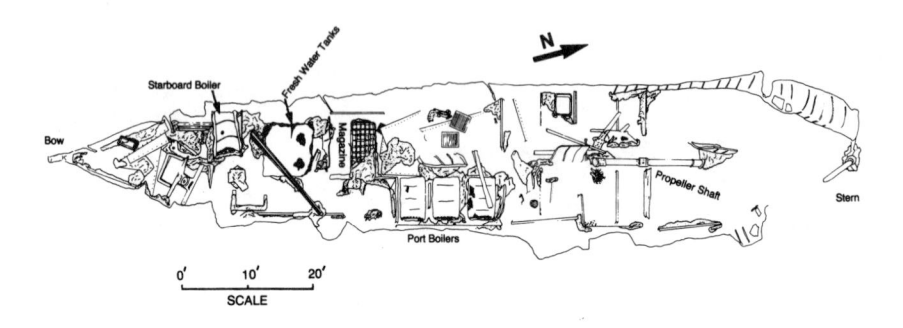

**Figure 4.** *Huron* site plan based on the 1987 and 1988 field investigations (graphic by J. Friday).

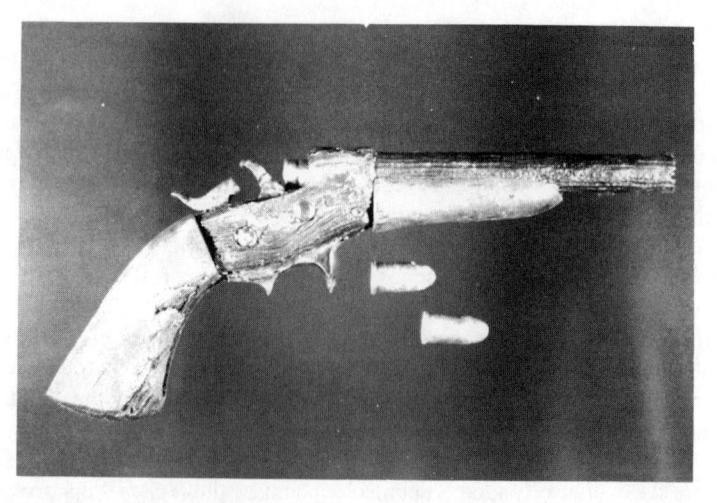

**Figure 5.** A fifty-caliber Remington rolling-block pistol recovered from the site during the 1987 field project.

## 3. DESIGNATION AS A HISTORIC SHIPWRECK PRESERVE

During the same period that Sanderson and Friday conducted their investigations of the *Huron*, the U.S. Congress was attempting to resolve the longstanding debate over the ownership and jurisdiction of historic shipwrecks. The result of that deliberation was the enactment, on April 28, 1988, of the Abandoned Shipwreck Act of 1987 (Public Law 100-298). That important piece of legislation gave the states title to historic shipwrecks located on their submerged lands and called on the states to establish programs to manage those shipwrecks. In North Carolina, that responsibility fell to the Underwater Archaeology Unit (UAU), an agency within the Department of Cultural Resources' Division of Archives and History. At the time the Abandoned Shipwreck Act was enacted, the UAU had been managing shipwrecks within the territorial waters of North Carolina for over twenty years under the authority of a state statute "Salvage of Abandoned Shipwrecks and other Underwater Archaeological Sites" (NCGS 121 Article 3). In passing the Abandoned Shipwreck Act, the U.S. Congress recognized that "...shipwrecks offer recreational and educational opportunities to sport divers and other interested groups..." Further, the law recommended that the states "...create underwater parks or areas to provide additional protection for such resources."

In North Carolina, the staff of the UAU was intrigued by the idea of designating a shipwreck park somewhere in the state's waters and immediately focused attention on the *Huron*. There were several reasons why the *Huron* was selected to become the state's first preserve: 1) the shipwreck was already a popular dive site; 2) the vessel had an interesting and significant history; 3) the town of Nags Head was interested in the project and willing to provide material assistance and site monitoring; and 4) the site had undergone extensive historical and archaeological documentation. Before the UAU could proceed with a designation, however, there were several issues to be resolved. First, there was no existing program or mechanism for designating a site as a shipwreck park or preserve. Second, there was concern about what liability the state would assume by such a designation. Third, since the *Huron* was a former Navy vessel, any action involving the site would have to be approved by the U.S. Navy. Finally, the question remained as to who would monitor day-to-day activities at the shipwreck and maintain buoys and exhibits, and how any site development would be funded.

In an effort to address those concerns, the UAU turned to two states, Vermont and Florida, which by 1989 were already operating successful shipwreck parks. Giovanna Peebles from Vermont and Roger Smith from Florida provided much needed information on their programs. In November 1989, members of the UAU, accompanied by Sandy Sanderson representing the town of Nags Head, traveled to Florida to meet with Roger Smith. While in Florida, the North Carolina team made a dive on the wreck of the *San*

*Pedro*, at that time one of Florida's two Underwater Archaeological Preserves.

Bolstered by the information from Peebles and Smith, and enthused by the dive on the *San Pedro*, the UAU staff prepared a proposal to create a "Historic Shipwreck Preserve" in North Carolina (Lawrence, 1990). The proposal recommended following Vermont's example to create a preserve system within the existing framework of laws and administrative procedures in order to avoid the time-consuming process of enacting new statutes and regulations. In reviewing North Carolina's laws pertaining to the Division of Archives and History, it appeared that there was sufficient statutory authority to designate a shipwreck site as a preserve with the expressed purpose of: 1) making the site more accessible to the general public; 2) interpreting the historical significance of the site; and 3) promoting the preservation of the site. In order to make the designation of the USS *Huron* Historic Shipwreck Preserve "official" the UAU presented a proposal to the North Carolina Historical Commission for their review. With the Historical Commission's enthusiastic endorsement, the Secretary of the Department of Cultural Resources issued a proclamation declaring the *Huron* to be an "Area of Primary Scientific/Historical Value" as set forth in North Carolina Administrative Code (T07:04R.1009.) Further, the proclamation designated the site as an historic shipwreck preserve with the stated goals of increasing public access, historical interpretation, and site preservation.

In considering the issue of liability, the UAU found a 1981 opinion from the Vermont's Attorney General's Office very useful. Simply stated, that opinion concluded that since divers were currently allowed to visit state-owned shipwrecks, the state already assumed a degree of liability. That liability might increase somewhat if the state actually encouraged divers to visit a site as in the case of a shipwreck park. However, as long as conditions on the site were no more hazardous than what were normally encountered in scuba diving, or if divers were warned of hazardous conditions, the state's assumption of additional liability would be minimal. The North Carolina Attorney General's Office reviewed the Vermont opinion and concurred with its findings.

Although the Abandoned Shipwreck Act gave the states title to historic shipwrecks, the *Huron* was an exception since it was a former Navy vessel. In 1990, the UAU entered into a dialogue with the Naval Historical Center (NHC) regarding the management of U.S. Navy shipwrecks in North Carolina waters. When the UAU approached the Navy about the possibility of designating the *Huron* as a shipwreck preserve, the Director of Naval History, Dean Allard, and Senior Naval Historian, William Dudley, offered their wholehearted support. Eventually, the Department of Cultural Resources entered into a Memorandum of Agreement with the U.S. Navy that allowed the state to designate and maintain the *Huron* site as a shipwreck preserve. The agreement also required the department to submit an annual report to the NHC detailing the status of the preserve, visitation figures, and any observable

# USS *HURON* PRESERVE

impacts or changes to the site.

The most crucial element in creating the *Huron* Historic Shipwreck Preserve was not the one-time act of designating the preserve, but rather determining who would be responsible for the long-term, day-to-day management of the shipwreck. In his advice to the UAU, Florida State Underwater Archeologist Roger Smith emphasized that for a shipwreck park program to be successful it must have the backing and support of the local community. In the case of the *Huron*, the town of Nags Head played the key role in making the idea of a shipwreck park a reality. From the beginning town officials, including Ocean Rescue Director Sandy Sanderson, Town Manager J. Webb Fuller, Mayor Donald Bryan, and the entire town council, were strongly in favor of the shipwreck park concept. In May of 1991, the Department of Cultural Resources entered into a formal agreement with the town of Nags Head detailing the responsibilities of both parties. In that document the town agreed to maintain two buoys on the site during the diving season, make monthly inspections of the shipwreck to note any changes to the site or hazardous conditions, monitor divers swimming out to and returning from the site, keep track of visitation figures, and develop an interpretive exhibit at the Bladen Street Beach Access (Figure 6). In addition to municipal

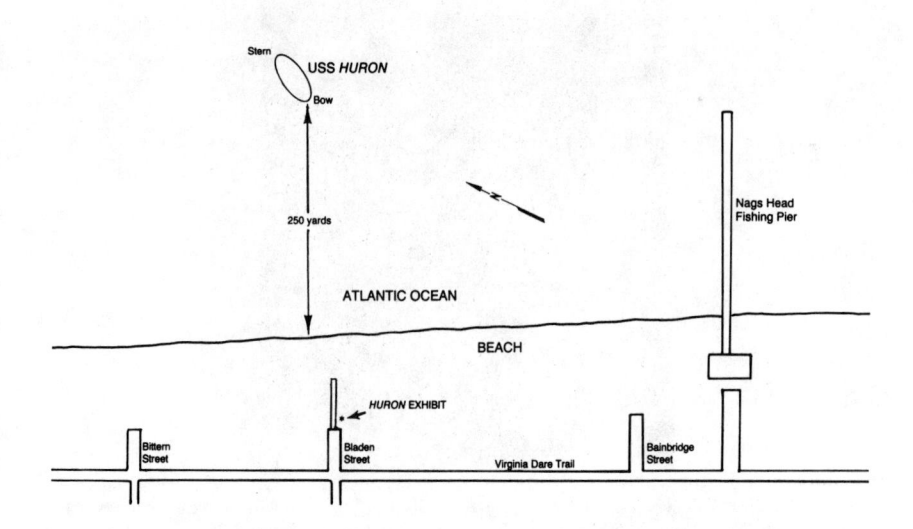

**Figure 6.** USS *Huron* Historic Shipwreck Preserve location map.

support, a local nonprofit group, the Outer Banks Community Foundation, provided a generous $3,000 grant that was used to construct an exhibit gazebo at the Bladen Street Beach Access. The grant also paid for printing an interpretive brochure, constructing a traveling exhibit on the *Huron*, and placing an underwater commemorative marker. The North Carolina Army National Guard provided a helicopter to transport the marker to the shipwreck site.

On November 24, 1991, at a beachside ceremony, Cultural Resources Secretary Patric Dorsey officially designated the *Huron* as North Carolina's first historic shipwreck preserve. After remarks from Secretary Dorsey, Nags Head Mayor Donald Bryan and U.S. Navy Commander P. C. Dorsey cut a ribbon to open the exhibit gazebo, and Nags Head Ocean Rescue divers placed a wreath on the wreck site in tribute to the seamen who lost their lives on the *Huron* (Figure 7).

**Figure 7.** From left: Commander P.C. Dorsey, USN (ret.), Cultural Resources Secretary Patric Dorsey, and Nags Head Mayor Donald Bryan cut the ribbon to open the *Huron* exhibit gazebo, November 24, 1991.

## 4. CONCLUSION

In the decade between 1991 and 2001, an estimated three thousand divers visited the wreck of the *Huron*. The marker buoys maintained by the town made it much easier for those divers to swim out and locate the shipwreck. In addition, the interpretive displays and brochures enhanced the diver's understanding of the various features of the wreck as well as the ship's history. During that decade there was only one reported incident--the recovery of a porthole in 1992--of a diver removing an artifact from the site. When that diver returned to shore, the artifact was confiscated by a lifeguard and turned over to the UAU for conservation.

In addition to divers, an untold number of beachgoers have benefited from the exhibit signs in the beachside gazebo. At that exhibit visitors have learned about the history of the *Huron* and its tragic sinking. From the end of the boardwalk they have gazed out to the ocean and viewed the buoys marking the bow and stern of the shipwreck. The fact that nearly one hundred sailors lost their lives on that stormy night in November 1877, despite the relative closeness of the shore, speaks dramatically to the awesome force of nature. In that respect, the *Huron* disaster can be viewed as representative of a scene that has repeated itself thousands of times along this treacherous stretch of coastline popularly known as the "Graveyard of the Atlantic." Yet, despite the tragedy of the *Huron*'s loss, two positive events have resulted from the vessel's sinking. First, in the 1870s public outcry over the *Huron* tragedy prompted a reluctant Congress to appropriate funds to expand the U.S. Lifesaving Service. Second, one hundred and fourteen years after the ship's loss, the site was designated as a "living" museum where the public can experience firsthand this dramatic and intriguing episode of the nation's rich maritime past.

## REFERENCES

Coletta, P., 1987, *The American Naval Heritage*, University Press of America, New York.
Friday, J., 1988, *A History of the Wreck of the USS Huron*, unpublished master's thesis, East Carolina University, Greenville, North Carolina.
Friday, J., and Lawrence, R., 1991, *USS* Huron *National Register of Historic Places Registration Form*, manuscript on file, Underwater Archaeology Unit, Kure Beach, North Carolina.
Lawrence, R., 1990, *A Review of the Shipwreck Preserve System and Recommendations for the Creation of the USS* Huron *Shipwreck Preserve in North Carolina*, manuscript on file, Underwater Archaeology Unit, Kure Beach, North Carolina.
Means, D., 1987, A heavy sea running; the formation of the U.S. Life Saving Service, 1848–1878, *Prologue, Journal of the National Archives*, Volume XIX, Number 4.

CHAPTER 6

# THE VISITOR SCHEMES ON THE HISTORIC SHIPWRECKS OF THE *SWAN* AND HMS *DARTMOUTH*, SOUND OF MULL, SCOTLAND (UK)

Philip Robertson[*]

## 1. INTRODUCTION

Diving in United Kingdom (UK) waters is a challenge. Cold water and fast-changing weather patterns are to be expected together with varying degrees of underwater visibility and wildly fluctuating tidal diving windows. Nevertheless, diving is very popular and there are approximately one hundred and twenty thousand active divers in the UK (UK CEED, 2000). British waters are not short of attractions for divers. Gray skies overhead hint little of rich marine habitats underwater (Gubbay, 1988). British seas also conceal the secrets of an island nation, until recently dependent on sea transport for survival. Current estimates suggest that between four thousand and sixty-five hundred wrecks exist around the coast of Scotland, though the work of private researchers suggests that as many as twenty thousand maritime casualties have occurred since the mid-eighteenth century (Oxley, 2001).

Several exciting initiatives have been set up to ensure that although the sea remains in the minds of most Britons, it need not remain out of sight. The snorkel trail at Lundy Marine Nature Reserve (Irving and Gilliland, 1998) is one example of several marine nature trails providing interpretation for those willing to get wet. Roving Eye Enterprises' R.O.V. trips for tourists in Orkney, and *Seaprobe Atlantis*, a glass-bottom boat visiting wildlife sites and a

---

[*] Philip Robertson, Nautical Archaeology Training (Training in Scotland), Lochaline Dive Center, Lochaline, Movern, Argyll, PA34 5XT, Scotland, United Kingdom.

shallow shipwreck in Skye, show that non-divers, too, can glimpse what lies under the waves in UK waters (Oxley, 2001).

Tourist access to archaeological sites and monuments on land is now standard practice (English Heritage, 1988). A shortage of funds to conserve raised ships for display in museums and a shift in management policy towards conserving marine archaeology *in situ* (Gregory, 1999) reinforce the need for innovative schemes to facilitate non-damaging tourist access to the UK's most important shipwreck sites. The UK Government's Department for Culture, Media and Sport has funded installation of interpretation boards on land adjacent to selected historic wreck sites in England and interpretation of intertidal shipwrecks for non-divers is not uncommon (Robertson, 1992). This paper discusses the aims, methodology, and results of the *Swan* and HMS *Dartmouth* Visitor Schemes in the Sound of Mull, Scotland. These two case studies are examined in the context of UK legislation and public attitudes relating to the discovery and preservation of the underwater heritage.

## 2. SHIPWRECK LEGISLATION AND ATTITUDES TOWARDS SHIPWRECK HERITAGE MANAGEMENT

The UK has an undistinguished record in relation to the management of its underwater heritage to date (Fenwick and Gale, 1998). Although attitudes are beginning to change, a culture of souvenir hunting amongst British divers has taken its toll and many of the UK's best known shipwrecks have been stripped bare of artifacts. The legislative framework relating to the protection of the underwater heritage in the UK has done little to encourage the conservation of shipwreck sites. For example, the Merchant Shipping Act 1995 places emphasis on the ownership and disposal of artifacts recovered from the sea and pertains even to historic shipwrecks (Oxley, 2001). The UK's principal historic wreck legislation, the Protection of Wrecks Act 1973, was enacted to safeguard wrecks of historical, archaeological, or artistic importance, yet it seems clear that the 1973 Bill was intended to facilitate recovery of archaeological material rather than to ensure conservation of wreck sites (Firth, 1999).

Reviews (JNAPC, 2000) have pointed out deficiencies in this statute and improvements were made to the statute which, when passed through parliament, were seen as a first step (Firth, 1999). While Historic Scotland has recently stated that underwater archaeology should be treated no differently than terrestrial archaeology in Scotland's waters (Historic Scotland, 1999), the Protection of Wrecks Act 1973 confers no statutory responsibility to any agency to fund work on designated sites (Fenwick and Gale, 1998). Moreover, the 1973 Act does not facilitate non-damaging public access to designated sites (JNAPC, 2000:8).

Once passed through parliament, the Protection of Wrecks Act 1973 empowered state authorities in England, Wales, Scotland, and Northern Ireland to designate by order a restricted area around the site of a vessel lying on, or in, the seabed of UK waters (excluding the Isle of Man and Channel Islands). In Scotland, the responsibilities of the Secretary of State for Scotland in the conservation of the underwater heritage passed to Scottish ministers, under the terms of the Scotland Act 1998 (Historic Scotland, 1999). At this writing, seven wrecks in Scottish waters are designated under the Protection of Wrecks Act 1973.

Under the Protection of Wrecks Act 1973, it is an offense to tamper with, damage, or remove any part of the wreck of a designated vessel or its contents or former contents, to carry out diving or salvage operations, or to deposit anything which would obliterate or obstruct access to the site. Activity on designated sites can only be undertaken under the authority of a license, currently issued in Scotland by Historic Scotland as the Scottish parliament's agency. Until 1994, two categories of license were available (Dean et al., 1999):

- Survey licenses were intended to cover non-intrusive site investigation involving survey and recording without disturbance to the site.
- Excavation licenses allow disturbance of a site. This would not normally be granted without submission of a completed pre-disturbance survey to the supervisory body, the Advisory Committee on Historic Wreck Sites (ACHWS).

The lack of any provision for public access has been very unpopular with the recreational diving public, who are responsible for locating approximately 50% of the nation's historic shipwrecks (Firth, 1999). By the mid 1990s, it was becoming clear that these two categories of license did not adequately cover the full range of activities which could, and should, be carried out on designated sites without any damage being done.

## 3. SOUND OF MULL VISITOR SCHEMES

The Sound of Mull is a twenty mile strait of water separating the island of Mull from mainland Scotland. Castles situated at strategic points on the coastline confirm the importance of the Sound as a seaway since at least A.D. 1200. Records suggest that more than sixty ships have been lost since the seventeenth century when records began. The Sound's clear waters and intact wrecks attract divers and the area is one of Scotland's top two wreck diving destinations. Divers have been responsible for locating many of the approximately fifteen known shipwrecks. The earliest identified shipwrecks date to the mid-seventeenth century, but the majority of sites date from the nineteenth and twentieth centuries. The two seventeenth century wrecks, the *Swan* and HMS *Dartmouth*, are designated under the Protection of Wrecks Act 1973.

Since 1994, the Nautical Archaeology Society (NAS) has based much of its Scottish field training activities in the area. In 1994, The Nautical Archaeology Society's inaugural Sound of Mull Archaeological Project (SOMAP) field school took place in cooperation with the Archaeological Diving Unit based at the University of St Andrews. Training activities coincided with summer fieldwork on the nearby historic wreck of the *Swan* at Duart Point (Martin, 1995). At the suggestion of the licensee, and with strong support from Historic Scotland, the ACHWS approved a pilot project proposal for a visitor scheme enabling field school participants to dive on the *Swan* under supervision during the fieldwork season.

In 1995, the ACHWS approved an application to broaden the visitor scheme concept inviting any sport diver, not just those with basic archaeological qualifications, to visit the *Swan* under appropriate supervision. The administration of the license required prior written notification to Historic Scotland of the names of all divers to be included on the visitor license. Three open days were arranged to coincide with the summer field season on the site. Sixty five visitors participated on these open days.

Between 1995 and 1996, the scheme was administered by the author, unofficially on behalf of the NAS and Historic Scotland. In 1996, I became the owner of Lochaline Dive Centre, a small center offering accommodation, air, and boat moorings for visiting divers. From 1997 until the present, the scheme has been administered as part of the field training activities of NAS Training (Scotland), which, since 1997, has had its headquarters at Lochaline Dive Centre. NAS Training in Scotland is grant-assisted by Historic Scotland. This grant provides for the running of training courses throughout Scotland during the winter. In the summer months, activities concentrate in the Sound of Mull where trainees can practice their skills in real situations. The Visitor Schemes have become an important part of NAS Scotland's overall training package, offering a window into underwater archaeology and diving on historic shipwrecks. While the training scheme is grant supported, historic wreck trips are funded by paying customers. The income generated from the scheme has been an important factor in NAS Scotland's efforts to promote underwater archaeology throughout Scotland and beyond.

Since 1995, the Visitor Scheme has operated each year with increasing participant numbers. By the end of 2000, a total of five hundred and forty-two divers have visited the *Swan*, and some have been twice. Following the success of the *Swan* Visitor Scheme, an application was made in 1996 to set up a similar scheme on the nearby designated site of HMS *Dartmouth*. This scheme was managed along similar lines to the *Swan* Visitor Scheme. To date, three hundred and thirty-seven visitors have participated in the HMS *Dartmouth* open days. Attendance numbers on both visitor licenses are given in Table 1.

Elsewhere in the UK, a limited visitor scheme was subsequently set up in 1996 on the wreck of SS *Iona II,* located within the boundaries of Lundy Marine Nature Reserve (Robertson and Heath, 1997). During 1997, the success of the *Swan* and HMS *Dartmouth* schemes led to a review of the categories of license issued to dive on designated sites (ACHWS, 1997:5). The review concluded that two additional categories of license should be issued where appropriate. One of these, the Visitor License, allowed for visiting sites where there is no active archaeological work proposed.

In the years following, local groups in England took up the challenge and a Visitor License was approved for the wreck of the *Resurgam* in 1998. The picture looks promising following final approval of the expanded license scheme in 2000. The Hampshire and Wight Trust for Maritime Archaeology's opening of a visitor trail on the wreck of the *Hazardous* on the South Coast of England has been universally welcomed (Momber and Satchell, 2001).

## 3.1. *Swan* Visitor Scheme

The *Swan* shipwreck is located at the southeastern entrance to the Sound of Mull on a rocky promontory beneath Duart Castle, seat of the Clan Maclean. The wreck dates to a September 1653 expedition sent by Oliver Cromwell to combat pockets of Royalist resistance to parliamentarian rule which existed in the Western Isles (Martin, 1995). The wreck was designated under the Protection of Wrecks Act 1973 in 1992. It is carefully monitored by the residents and caretakers of Duart Castle who formed a liaison with the Coastguard, the Police, and the licensee. The advantages of this are considerable and there have been few reported incidents of unlicensed diving. This may be partly due to the publicity the Visitor Scheme has achieved through media coverage, and locally through cooperation with diving businesses in the Oban and Sound of Mull area.

Table 1. Visitor numbers on Sound of Mull visitor schemes.

|      | HMS *Dartmouth* |         |
| ---- | --------------- | ------- |
| Year | Visitor numbers | License |
| 1994 | N/A             | No      |
| 1995 | N/A             | No      |

| 1996 | 18 | Yes |
| 1997 | 0 | Yes |
| 1998 | 136 | Yes |
| 1999 | 108 | Yes |
| 2000 | 85 | Yes |
| **Total** | **337** | |

| *Swan* | | |
|---|---|---|
| Year | Visitor numbers | License |
| 1994 | 17 | Yes |
| 1995 | 65 | Yes |
| 1996 | 58 | Yes |
| 1997 | 44 | Yes |
| 1998 | 136 | Yes |
| 1999 | 101 | Yes |
| 2000 | 121 | Yes |
| **Total** | **542** | |

Following an initial rescue operation to recover threatened artifacts in 1992, a comprehensive pre-disturbance survey completed a site plan of the site and preceded a program of site stabilization. Sandbags were laid over the structural timbers and over other unstable sections of the wreck site. These sandbags have become established as part of the site environment, largely obscuring ship remains beneath. While conducive as a method for preserving this wreck *in situ*, these sandbags are initially frustrating to visitors who want to see the wreck fully exposed. However, when the reasons for sandbagging are explained, most visitors fully accept this situation.

The *Swan* lies in ten to twelve meters of water and a tidal diving window of approximately six hours means that the *Swan* is not limited to only experienced divers (Figure 1). For normal safety reasons, divers are asked to hold a CMAS 1* certificate or its equivalent. However, good buoyancy control is a prerequisite and the need to prevent disturbance of delicate deposits by ensuring good diving practices is stressed.

Figure 1. Diver underwater on the *Swan* (photo by C. Martin).

Historic wreck trips begin with a slide talk. This is useful for pointing out what divers will see and what they will not see, and for explaining the history of the ship and the ongoing archaeological work. Groups of up to twelve people visit the site although, where possible, numbers on the seabed are limited to six persons at any one time. Dives are preceded by a briefing covering basic safety advice in addition to three specific requests: visitors are asked not to remove artifacts; not to interfere with any part of the shipwreck or survey equipment; and to maintain good buoyancy control at all times (Figure 2). No direct supervision of the divers is applied underwater; trust and peer-pressure are considered effective guarantees of responsible conduct.

The first open days were carried out at times when the field team was at work and the structural features of the ship were visible. The presence of survey grids, planning frames, and equipment such as current meters enhanced the wreck as a visitor attraction. Participants expressed particular pleasure at being able to see the wooden hull structure of such an old ship, not something that any of them had previously experienced. In 1996, the hull structure was covered up following the completion of the pre-disturbance survey. This had a marked effect in the enjoyment experienced by visitors, although feedback remained very positive, and the opportunity of seeing a cast iron gun and anchor underwater from a three hundred year old wreck satisfied the majority.

On the *Swan*, interpretive aids were placed on the seabed, partly as a guide to maximize the educational potential of each visit, but also as a control to limit unguided access to less stable parts of the site. Visitors may carry a copy of the site plan with the trail marked on it. The trail consists of a rope line guiding visitors on a tour around the most visible features of the shipwreck.

**Figure 2.** Briefing visitors before their dive (photo by C. Martin).

Signposts, used to point out particular features, are made of yellow plastic tied to lead weights on the seabed or attached with light line to large structures such as cast iron guns. In this way, the signs were designed to float above the seabed with minimum impact to the site itself. Signs are useful in drawing attention to objects which might otherwise not be noticed, such as stone ballast, and to other features for which some explanation is required, such as the aluminum anodes used to conserve the site's larger iron features including the guns and anchor. Feedback from participants does not suggest that visitors found the signposting intrusive, or that it spoilt their sense of discovery. However, the desire for discovery may explain why many divers opt not to take the site plans with them. Even with signposting, site plans, and a shot line guiding them to the start of the trail, buddy pairs have occasionally missed the wreck altogether. Such signposting, however, demands constant maintenance and is therefore a demand on specialized diver time.

Back on dry land, open days include a tour around Duart Castle where there is an exhibition about the wreck. Participants end their day with a special stamp in their logbook and a leaflet about the wreck--souvenirs of authenticity which the visitors appreciate particularly. The *Swan* project team have made separate efforts to provide interpretation about the wreck for the non-diving public (Martin, 1998). Historic Scotland funded the erection of a wreck information board located on the rock promontory above the *Swan*, which has proved very popular with passers-by. During the filming of a BBC documentary about the project, the team experimented with the use of fish farm monitoring cameras linked by hard wire to a surface monitor. The potential of this system as a cost-effective method of demonstrating work on the seabed to tourists is clear.

## 3.2. HMS *Dartmouth* Visitor Scheme

The wreck of the fifth-rate Royal Navy Frigate HMS *Dartmouth* lies in shallow water (two to ten meters) off the island of Eilean Rubha an Ridire, close to the Morvern shore of the Sound of Mull (Figure 3). The wreck was identified by divers visiting the nearby iron wreck of the *Ballista* in 1973 and was surveyed and excavated during the late 1970s by the University of St. Andrews (Martin, 1978). Existing seabed remains include considerable amount of remaining hull structure, three anchors, and seventeen cast iron guns. The wreck was designated under the Protection of Wrecks Act 1973 in 1973, although this designation was revoked in 1979. However, the growth of sport diving in the Sound of Mull and the proximity of the wreck to the popular *Ballista*, meant that the ship was under threat from souvenir hunters.

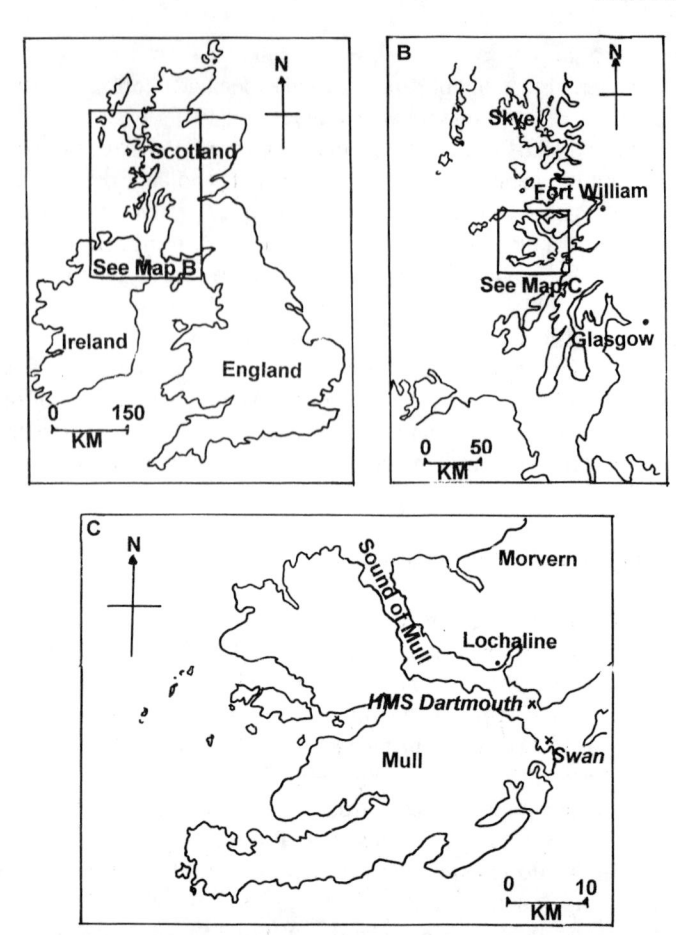

**Figure 3.** Maps of Great Britain and Ireland, western Scotland (1B), and the Sound of Mull (1C). The wreck was re-designated in June 1992, and re-surveyed during SOMAP 1994 by NAS volunteers (Diamond, 1994).

Numerous instances of unlicensed tourist diving occur on the HMS *Dartmouth*. The isolation of the wreck site and its proximity to an unprotected site are all contributory factors. In an effort to facilitate legal and controllable tourist access to the HMS *Dartmouth*, an application was made and accepted in 1996 to set an official visitor scheme on the wreck.

During spring, kelp coverage of the site is minimal but, as the season progresses, substantial growth of kelp over the site occurs, with coverage reaching a peak by August. Kelp is advantageous in terms of protecting the shipwreck and its environment, both from illegal diver access and by assisting in the creation of a stable burial environment. However, kelp growth hindered visitor access, causing practical problems, particularly in the setting-up and maintenance of the trail. It diminished visitors' appreciation of the wreck site because even the larger objects such as guns and anchors became increasingly difficult to identify. If visitors have nothing to see, a potentially exciting dive is turned into a negative visitor experience. Several participants felt that it confirmed their worst fears, namely that archaeology really is boring.

In 1999, the ACHWS granted permission to begin a pilot project to cut kelp on the HMS *Dartmouth* site to improve the wreck for visiting divers. The agreed plan was preceded by consultation with marine biologists and archaeologists. Its objectives were to improve visitors' enjoyment of their dive by conducting a limited clearance of kelp on the visitor trail in such a way that minimized damage to the wreck and its environment. A program of limited kelp cutting was carried out between May and August when kelp growth reaches its peak.

Kelp was cut only at selected points on the wreck site (Figure 4). The defined areas are two squares (twenty square meters and twenty-five square meters) containing the major concentrations of the ship's iron guns and the main anchor, and a path one meter either side of the trail marker rope following a line of cannon towards the northwest end of the site. The maximum area of cleared kelp was estimated to be seventy-five square meters. Kelp was cut by knife at a point approximately fifteen centimeters above the holdfast. Where possible, cut kelp was disposed of away from the wreck site by making use of favorable currents near the site.

The following environmental impacts were envisaged, and kelp cutting planned in such a way as to mitigate unnecessary impacts:

- Cutting would clearly denude a localized area of kelp growth during the trial period. However, the resident kelp species--consisting mostly of *Laminaria digitata*--re-grows annually and, on completion of the trial, it was foreseen that kelp growth levels should return to pre-project levels fairly quickly.
- Kelp supports macrofauna communities on its stem and fronds and a localized impact to these communities is unavoidable. Yet, the majority of these animal communities are concentrated mostly in the holdfast area and, by cutting plants above the holdfast, the impact on these communities could be minimized.
- It is known that kelp does have an effect on the current systems over the wreck site and the effects of this could be considerable. To monitor any effects on the stability of the shipwreck and seabed sediments, a program of corrosion monitoring was carried out.

The effects of kelp clearance were assessed as part of an NAS-supported research project (Cook and Kaye, 2000). Seabed monitoring stakes were embedded in sediment at different points over the site at the start of the dive season and then collected at the end of the season. Analysis of the collected stakes enabled researchers to conclude that corrosivity of sediment across the site was uniform and unaffected by the presence or absence of kelp.

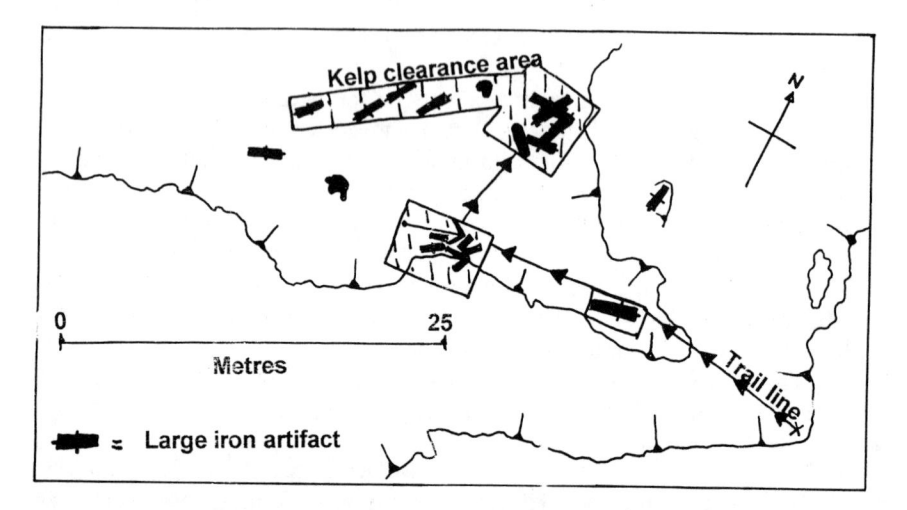

**Figure 4.** Map showing trail line and kelp cutting zones on HMS *Dartmouth*.

There was evidence for increased corrosivity at deeper points on the site but this was attributed to increased tidal flow resulting in raised oxygenation. The research team concluded "kelp clearance had no effect on the archaeology over the monitored period" (Cook and Kaye, 2000:7).

## 4. CONCLUSIONS

Based on visual monitoring of the Scheme to date, no incidents of damage to archaeology resulting from visitor access have been noted. Conclusions on the effectiveness of the Visitor Schemes as a public access and education tool are based purely on informal feedback from participants. The opportunity to dive on an historic shipwreck is something which has been appreciated by all participants, while opinions of the enjoyment of diving on these two sites vary from real satisfaction, particularly when dives have coincided with ongoing fieldwork, to dissatisfaction at the limited amount of visible artifacts. The Visitor Schemes have been popular amongst the local dive charter operators who have been able to bring their own groups to dive the historic shipwrecks through the Visitor Scheme system. It is clear, therefore, that the Schemes have been invaluable in helping to break down the sense of exclusion which recreational divers have felt in relation to historic shipwrecks.

The Visitor Scheme concept may not be suitable for every historic wreck. For instance, less robust sites where organic deposits are at risk from extensive diver activity would not be good candidates for Visitor Scheme access. Similarly, sites situated in high-risk diving environments would be no more suitable. Nevertheless, it must be hoped that the Visitor Scheme concept will be taken up on more historic wreck sites in UK waters and elsewhere. It is also hoped that the mechanics of the licensing system can be simplified with responsibilities for approving access to each individual to be devolved to the site licensee. This would reduce the considerable administrative burden placed on heritage agencies and licensees if the scheme continues to grow as expected.

## ACKNOWLEDGEMENTS

Thanks to Dr. Colin Martin, Dr. Paula Martin, and Mr. Ian Oxley for their helpful comments and assistance in relation to this paper, and to Dr. Colin Martin for permission to reproduce photographs.

# REFERENCES

Advisory Committee on Historic Wreck Sites (ACHWS),1997, *Annual Report*, Department of Culture Media and Sport, London.
Cook, J., and Kaye, B., 2000, A new method for monitoring site stability in situ, *Nautical Archaeology Society Newsletter* 2000(4):7.
Dean, M., Lawrence, M., Liscoe, S., Oxley, I., Wood, A., 1999, *Protected Historic Wrecks, Guidance Notes for Divers and Archaeologists*, Archaeological Diving Unit, University of St Andrews, St Andrews.
Diamond, P., 1994, The Dartmouth, NAS Part II Survey Project, Nautical Archaeology Society, Portsmouth.
English Heritage, 1988, *Visitors Welcome*, London.
Fenwick, V., and Gale, A., 1998, *Historic Shipwrecks:Discovered, Protected and Investigated*, Tempus, Stroud.
Firth, A., 1999, Making archaeology: the history of the protection of Wrecks Act 1973 and the constitution of an archaeological resource, *International Journal of Nautical Archaeology* 28(1):10-24.
Gregory,D., 1999, Monitoring the effect of sacrificial anodes on the large iron artefacts on the Duart Point Wreck 1997, *International Journal of Nautical Archaeology* 28(2):164-175.
Gubbay, S., 1988, *Coastal Directory for Marine Nature Conservation*, Marine Conservation Society, Gloucester.
Historic Scotland, 1999, *Conserving the Underwater Heritage*. Historic Scotland Operational Policy Paper HP.6, Historic Scotland, Edinburgh.
Irving, R., and Gilliland, P., 1998, Lundy's Marine Nature Reserve, a short history, in: *Island studies, Fifty Years of the Lundy Field Society*, R. Irving, J. Schofield, and C. Webster, eds., Devon, pp.185-203.
JNAPC, 2000, *Heritage Law at Sea*, University of Wolverhampton, Wolverhampton, UK
Martin, C., 1978, The Dartmouth, a British frigate wrecked off Mull, 1690, in: The Ship, *International Journal of Nautical Archaeology* 7(1): 9-58.
Martin, C., 1995, A Cromwellian shipwreck off Duart Point, Mull: an interim report, *International Journal of Nautical Archaeology* 24(1):15-32.
Martin, C., 1998, *Scotland's Historic Shipwrecks*, Batsford, UK.
Momber, G., and Satchell, J., 2001, Having a trail of a time, *Nautical Archaeology Society Newsletter* 2001(4):1.
Oxley, I., 2001, Towards the integrated management of Scotland's cultural heritage: examining historic shipwrecks as marine environmental resources. *World Archaeology* 3(2):in press.
Robertson, P., 1992, The Seven Sisters Voluntary Marine Conservation Area: a Maritime Archaeological Perspective, M.Litt thesis, Scottish Institute of Maritime Studies, University of St Andrews, St. A.ndrews.
Robertson, P., and Heath, J., 1997, Marine Archaeology and Lundy, in: *Island studies, Fifty Years of the Lundy Field Society*, R. Irving, J. Schofield, and C. Webster, ed.,. Devon, pp.77-86.
UK CEED, 2000, *A Review of the Effects of Recreational Interactions Within UK Marine Sites*, Countryside Council for Wales (UK Marine SAC's Project), UK.

CHAPTER 7

# LAKE CHAMPLAIN'S UNDERWATER HISTORIC PRESERVE PROGRAM: REASONABLE ACCESS TO APPROPRIATE SITES

Arthur B. Cohn[*]

## 1. INTRODUCTION

What is the value of a shipwreck? Who owns shipwrecks in public waters, and who controls access to them? What type of access is reasonable? These issues have been evolving for Lake Champlain through the development of the Lake Champlain Underwater Historic Preserve Program during the past fifteen years. This underwater museum environment has proven to be an ideal testing ground for demonstrating how the archaeological community and sport divers can work together to ensure the preservation of submerged cultural resources in Lake Champlain.

## 2. HISTORY OF LAKE CHAMPLAIN'S PRESERVES

It is fair to say that Lake Champlain was better known in the eighteenth century world than it is today. The lake was an integral one hundred twenty-mile-long, north-south superhighway which allowed armies, navies, commercial goods, and travelers to move through the New England interior throughout the seventeenth, eighteenth, and nineteenth centuries. Today, the lake's military and commercial watercraft have been replaced by a fleet of recreational vessels, but archaeological remains continue to provide vivid reminders of the lake's rich history. As long as ships have been sailing on Lake Champlain, they have been sinking in Lake Champlain, and nothing fires

---

[*] Arthur B. Cohn, Executive Director, Lake Champlain Maritime Museum, 4472 Basin Harbor Road, Vergennes, Vermont 05491.

the public imagination like a shipwreck. In the past, many historic ships were raised from the lake for exhibit but no longer exist in any recognizable form, because without adequate conservation most of the ships eventually deteriorated.

Two decades ago, Kevin Crisman and the author undertook a new effort to locate the lake's shipwrecks and to document them with non-invasive underwater archaeological techniques. The steamboat *Phoenix*, launched in 1815 and burned in a violent fire in 1819, was studied. Today the hull lies in sixty feet of water at the bow and one hundred ten feet at the stern (Davison, 1981). *A.R. Noyes*, a nineteenth-century standard canal boat loaded with coal that sank in eighty feet of water in 1884, was documented; this vessel still contains remnants of the mules' towing equipment and coal shovel fragments (Lake Champlain's Underwater Historic Preserve System, 1996). Research was conducted on the *General Butler*, an 1862 sailing canal schooner that was battered against the Burlington breakwater during a violent December gale and sank intact in forty feet of water in 1876 (Cohn et al., 1996). As these wonderful shipwrecks were studied, public interest and diver curiosity grew. As results were made public, archaeologists and administrators realized that either some type of engineered access to the sites could be orchestrated, or that the sites would be left unsupervised for divers to locate and explore on their own.

## 3. DIVER ACCESS TO SHIPWRECKS

In 1985, *Phoenix*, *A.R. Noyes*, and *General Butler* became the first vessels in what was then the Vermont Underwater Historic Preserve Program. Administered by the Vermont Division for Historic Preservation, this program received its authorization from the 1975 Vermont Historic Preservation Act. Working with state archaeologist Giovanna Peebles, a program was designed to provide safe access to appropriate sites. In 1987, the Federal Abandoned Shipwreck Act formally gave the states title to shipwrecks in their waters and mandated reasonable diver access.

The most important feature of the Vermont Preserve system is a seasonal mooring, installed in the spring and removed in the fall, which allows divers to locate a shipwreck easily and to secure their boats at the surface. The need to drop anchors at the sites has been completely eliminated (Figure 1). Once a dive boat has been secured, the divers follow the mooring chain to an anchor pad and then follow a travel line to the wreck. Each wreck has signage on the bottom that identifies the site and requests divers' cooperation in preserving it.

The Coast Guard cooperated by installing the mooring anchors, and each site required a Coast Guard "Special Purpose Buoy" permit. A program brochure and individual site brochures were developed to inform divers of appropriate dive protocols and the history of each site. Over the next five

**Figure 1.** In 1985, the Lake Champlain Underwater Historic Preserve Program established its first moorings on three selected shipwrecks. The moorings permitted divers to locate the sites and to secure their boats to a large, visible special-purpose mooring ball. The mooring provided a safer diving mechanism and removed the need to drop anchors near the shipwreck.

years, the "gentle formality" of this program, designed to run on a state budget of $5,000 a year and "good intentions," provided a positive historical and recreational experience to thousands of regional and visiting divers. There were less than a handful of vandalism incidents, although over time the sites did show signs of wear and tear. Remarkably, since the program's inception, there have been no Preserve-related diving accidents.

## 4. BURLINGTON BAY HORSE FERRY

In 1989, National Geographic Magazine was preparing to run an article on the Burlington Bay Horse Ferry, the only known turntable-style horse ferry preserved in North America. This rare site had intentionally been excluded from the Preserve system because of concerns about its fragility and archaeological sensitivity. In response to heightened concerns about the implications that might result from national exposure and worried that divers would drop anchors to locate the wreck, a community committee discussed the issue. The decision was made to open the site as a Preserve in 1989 with the stipulation that this one-of-a-kind watercraft first be completely documented archaeologically. Over the next four years the site was recorded through an archaeological field school, sponsored by the Lake Champlain Maritime Museum, the University of Vermont, and Texas A&M University. After a decade of research, a book was published about the site and about the history of horse-powered watercraft in North America (Crisman and Cohn, 1998).

In 1989, in addition to the Burlington Bay Horse Ferry, another vessel, known as the Diamond Island Stone Boat, was added to the Preserve system. This wooden canal boat, similar in size and construction to the coal barge *A.R. Noyes,* had no independent means of propulsion and had sunk on the rocky shore of Diamond Island with its cargo of quarried stone blocks intact (Lake Champlain's Underwater Historic Preserve System, 1996).

## 5. UNDERWATER PRESERVE ADVISORY COMMITTEE

In the early 1990s, to manage the Preserve program better, the Underwater Preserve Advisory Committee was created. This ad-hoc committee, composed of members of the dive community, historians, archaeologists, and state officials, meets regularly to discuss issues facing the Preserves and makes recommendations to the Vermont Division for Historic Preservation. Underwater Preserve Monitors, trained personnel who provide on-site advice, information, and emergency services to visiting divers, were added on weekends from June through Labor Day. Working with a Preserve boat borrowed from the Vermont State Police, the program continues to operate on a state appropriation of $5,000 per year.

In 1996, an updated information booklet was published about the Underwater Preserves (Lake Champlain's Underwater Historic System, 1996) (Figure 2), which provides site history and dive protocols. At that time a new registration procedure was adopted, asking divers to register once each season. In this way, statistical information about program usage could be collected and administrators could be confident that all divers had received the information booklet.

## 6. ADDITION OF PRESERVE SITES

In 1998, the steamboat *Champlain II*, built in 1868, became New York's first underwater preserve site in Lake Champlain. In 1875 this vessel was run full-steam upon the shoreline; a subsequent investigation revealed that the

# Dive Historic Lake Champlain

Horse Ferry

## Lake Champlain's Underwater Historic Preserve System

State of Vermont • Division for Historic Preservation
New York State • Department of Environmental Conservation
* Version francaise disponible sur demand

**Figure 2.** The cover of the current Lake Champlain Underwater Historic Preserve System brochure.

steamboat's pilot was addicted to morphine. One hundred sixty feet of hull remains are now located in fifteen to thirty-five feet of water. The famous story of the shipwreck and its well-documented location meant that divers had known about *Champlain II* for years. However, its addition to the Preserves helped to protect the site by marking its location and providing a mooring buoy, thus diminishing the likelihood of anchor damage (Baldwin et al., 1996).

Also in 1998, the sailing canal schooner *O.J. Walker* became the program's seventh site (Figure 3). Although *O.J. Walker* had been located and studied in the 1980s, the decision was made at that time not to open the site. The ship was thirty-five years old when it sank, and its fragile condition was of great concern. At first only a few divers knew about the site, but each year more and more divers were observed attempting to locate and dive it. In 1996, during the site's annual inspection, divers discovered significant anchor damage to one of the masts and noted that the deck cabin's roof had been dislodged (Cohn et al., 1996). That winter the Underwater Preserve Advisory Committee deliberated the issue and recommended to the Vermont Division for Historic Preservation that the site be opened as a Preserve; funding was provided by the federally-authorized Lake Champlain Basin Program. The committee further recommended that, because of the fragile nature of the site,

**Figure 3.** Lake Champlain shipwrecks have been preserved by cold, fresh water and are remarkable intact. This figure shows the intact bow section and windlass of the sailing canal schooner *O.J. Walker*.

access be controlled by a new registration procedure. Divers would be required to sign up for a specific day and time in order to better monitor diver traffic. This procedure and a strong "zero-impact" diving protocol have worked extremely well, and *O.J. Walker* so far shows very little evidence of the hundreds of diver visits it has received.

Over the years, surface mooring hardware was improved and a new mooring system was installed. The Hazelett Elastic Mooring, designed in Vermont, provides a direct vertical descent/ascent line for the diver, eliminates the need for scope, and minimizes environmental impact to bottom sediments.

## 7. ASSESSING THE IMPACT OF ZEBRA MUSSELS ON UNDERWATER PRESERVE SITES

For decades everything learned about underwater preserves in Lake Champlain was good news, but in 1993 bad news arrived when zebra mussels were discovered in Lake Champlain. From their first inadvertent introduction to the lake, it was clear that zebra mussels would eventually encrust most of the lake's underwater cultural resources. Although the long-term effects of zebra mussels seemed to be dire, the future for Lake Champlain's shipwrecks could not be predicted with any certainty (Lake Champlain Management Conference, 1996). The Maritime Museum, in partnership with the University of Vermont, recently embarked on a new study designed to identify the actual impact of zebra mussels on the wood and iron of historic shipwrecks (Watzin et al., 2001).

The study of zebra mussels utilized six historic shipwreck sites and evaluated the chemistry of the water column just above the colony. In addition, multiple settlement tables were deployed at each site to facilitate zebra mussel colonies forming on the wood and iron samples, allowing the examination of the mussels' effect over time. Preliminary conclusions, based on the above, suggest that the iron components of historic shipwrecks are being degraded at a more rapid rate now that zebra mussels are present. This seems to be happening through creation of a micro-environment between the zebra mussel colony and the shipwreck. This zone appears to be an ideal environment for the growth of sulfur-reducing bacteria (SRBs), and the SRBs are the apparent cause of the iron degradation.

The arrival of zebra mussels pushed the Lake Champlain Maritime Museum to initiate an aggressive new lake survey to locate and document the lake's remaining shipwrecks before they became encrusted (McLaughlin and Lessman, 1998; Sabick et al., 2000). Utilizing state-of-the-art survey technology, over the past four years approximately one hundred sixty square miles of lake bottom have been examined and over forty previously unknown shipwrecks have been located. Most of the shipwrecks have been identified as nineteenth-century commercial vessels and many lie at depths less than one hundred feet. The survey's discovery of a large number of arguably "preserve-appropriate" shipwrecks is fueling the debate over the long-term potential and management of the Lake Champlain Underwater Preserve Program.

## 8. FUTURE MANAGEMENT OPTIONS

In 1999, the Lake Champlain Maritime Museum completed a new management study for the state of Vermont that directed the examination of the feasibility of turning the management of the state-run Preserve program over to a private, non-profit organization (Belisle and Cousins, 1999). The study decided that it might be possible, if issues surrounding legal liability and budgets could be resolved. The study also concluded that a unified program, one that would incorporate Preserve sites in both the states of Vermont and New York, would make the most sense. However, the complexity of New York's governmental bureaucracy (five agencies have jurisdiction over submerged cultural resources in New York compared to just one in Vermont), along with the traditional tension between the two states, which dates back to the days when Vermont's Ethan Allen was harassing New York surveyors, make undertaking a joint program a perplexing challenge.

In considering the future, a number of additional issues faces those working on Lake Champlain, and perhaps researchers in other regions as well. Should access be provided to interesting shallow-water historic sites in limited-visibility environments? Can divers be charged a user fee to help support the Preserve's operations? What access should be allowed to sites that are environmental concerns, such as a tugboat loaded with fuel oil? Should access be provided to a truly intact shipwreck, one still filled with artifacts? Must each site first be documented and its artifacts removed before public citizens can dive on it? How can these sites be better shared with the much larger non-diving public and how can school curricula be developed that will connect children to history and archaeology? New survey technology has the ability to find sites anywhere, and new technical diving techniques are expanding divers' ranges. What access should be granted to technical divers seeking pristine deep-water sites?

## 9. CONCLUSION

On Lake Champlain, a successful program has been created by providing access to a select number of depth-appropriate archaeological sites. The program has stimulated diver cooperation and has developed a preservation ethic within the diver community. The challenge now faced is managing the program to meet divers' expectations, while still preserving the integrity of archaeologically fragile sites. As survey and diving technology advances and becomes more readily available, these sites will be found and explored, with or without archaeologists.

Recently, the state of New York has commissioned a study on the feasibility of expanding their underwater preserve program. It is an encouraging development that has helped stimulate the federally funded Lake Champlain Basin Program to allocate funds for underwater preserve enhancement. Instituting a thoughtful, common-sense program now will help ensure safer access for divers and greater preservation of Lake Champlain's irreplaceable underwater cultural resources. There is a growing sense that the time is right to provide reasonable access to appropriate sites.

# REFERENCES

Baldwin, E. R., Cohn, A. B., Crisman, K. J. and McLaughlin, S. A., 1996, *Underwater Historic Preserve Feasibility Study of the Lake Champlain Steamboat Champlain II*, Lake Champlain Maritime Museum, Ferrisburg, Vermont.

Belisle, R. and Cousins, A., 1999, *The Lake Champlain Underwater Historic Preserve Management Plan for the Management of the Current and Future Underwater Preserve System*, Lake Champlain Maritime Museum, Ferrisburg, Vermont.

Cohn, A. B., Eddy, L., Petty, L., and Tichonuk, E., 1996, *Zebra Mussels and Their Impact on Historic Shipwrecks*, Lake Champlain Management Conference, Lake Champlain Maritime Museum, Ferrisburg, Vermont.

Cohn, A. B., Cozzi, J. R., Crisman, K. J., and McLaughlin, S. A., 1996, *The Archaeological Reconstruction of the Lake Champlain Canal Schooner General Butler*, Lake Champlain Maritime Museum, Ferrisburg, Vermont.

Ibid., 1996, *Underwater Preserve Feasibility Study of the Lake Champlain Canal Schooner O. J. Walker*, Lake Champlain Maritime Museum, Ferrisburg, Vermont.

Crisman, K. J. and Cohn, A. B., 1998, *When Horses Walked on Water: Horse-Powered Ferries in Nineteenth-Century America*, Smithsonian Institution Press, Washington and London.

Davison, R., 1981, *The Phoenix Project*, The Champlain Maritime Society, Burlington, Vermont.

Lake Champlain's Underwater Historic Preserve System, 1996, *Dive Historic Lake Champlain*, Lake Champlain Maritime Museum, Ferrisburg, Vermont.

McLaughlin, S. A. and Lessmann, A. W., 1998, *Lake Champlain Underwater Cultural Resources Survey*, Lake Champlain Maritime Museum, Ferrisburg, Vermont.

Sabick, C. R., Lessmann, A. W., and McLaughlin, S. A., 2000, *Lake Champlain Underwater Cultural Resources Survey*, Lake Champlain Maritime Museum, Ferrisburg, Vermont.

Watzin, M. C., Cohn, A. B., and Emerson, B. P., 2001, *Zebra Mussels, Shipwrecks and the Environment*, School of Natural Resources, University of Vermont, Burlington, Vermont.

CHAPTER 8

# FLORIDA'S UNDERWATER ARCHAEOLOGICAL PRESERVES

Della A. Scott-Ireton[*]

## 1. INTRODUCTION

Florida's numerous and varied waterways, including seas, bays, rivers, lakes, and springs, have been used for centuries for commerce, warfare, settlement, and travel. The result of this use is the deposition of cultural material, often wrecked and abandoned ships and boats, which can provide fascinating and important information about past cultures and lifeways. However, from the early days of hard-hat diving some of Florida's shipwrecks were mined for the artifacts they contained, resulting in a limited and superficial view of the value of submerged cultural resources. Florida's system of Underwater Archaeological Preserves represents an innovative method of public interpretation of shipwrecks and of submerged cultural resource management (Figure 1).

## 2. HISTORY OF FLORIDA'S PRESERVES

In the 1980s state underwater archaeologists with the Florida Division of Historical Resources embarked on a different path to encourage public appreciation of shipwrecks as non-renewable historical resources to be protected for future generations. Toward this end, one of the ships of the 1715 Spanish plate fleet, wrecked along Florida's east coast, was nominated to become the state's first Underwater Archaeological Preserve. *Urca de*

---

[*] Della A. Scott-Ireton, Bureau of Archaeological Research, Division of Historical Resources, Florida Department of State, 500 South Bronough Street, Tallahassee, Florida 32399-0250.

Figure 1. Florida's Underwater Archaeological Preserves are located around the state in a variety of settings and environments.

*Lima,* a flat-bottomed storeship belonging to Miguel de Lima, sank in shallow water near present-day Ft. Pierce. The first of this fleet found in the twentieth century, the vessel's cannons and anchors had long since been removed. Exposed timbers and associated ballast drew more divers than treasure hunters, prompting local government to form a partnership with the state to designate the site as Florida's first shipwreck Preserve in 1987. An experiment in cultural resource management, the Preserve proved to be popular with sport divers and is protected from further commercial salvage.

The success of the first Preserve inspired the Florida Department of State to expand this program. In the summer of 1988 Florida State University and Indiana University participated in a combined field school, under the direction of Florida's State Underwater Archaeologist, to survey the final resting places of the wrecked 1733 Spanish plate fleet. Scattered along eighty miles of the Florida Keys, most of these wrecks have been disturbed through salvage and relic collecting, although as dive sites they are picturesque with teeming sea life and colorful corals. Students relocated eleven wreck sites and evaluated them to determine which would make the best Preserve based on public accessibility, presence of sea life, archaeological features, and suitability for interpretation. The wreck of *San Pedro*, a Dutch-built galleon located off Islamorada, was chosen as the best candidate and designated the state's second Preserve in 1989.

For Florida's third Underwater Archaeological Preserve the wreck of the stern paddlewheel steamboat *City of Hawkinsville* proved to be a perfect candidate. Abandoned in 1921 and submerged along the bank of the Suwannee River near Old Town, *Hawkinsville* is amazingly well preserved. Steam machinery stands in place on the deck and paddlewheel spokes are visible in the murky water. With volunteer assistance and local support, the vessel was designated a Preserve in 1992.

In 1993 the nation's oldest existing battleship was established as Florida's fourth Underwater Archaeological Preserve. USS *Massachusetts* (BB2), launched in 1893 and active in the Spanish-American War, was sunk as a target ship off Pensacola in 1921. Resting in thirty feet of clear water with two large gun turrets awash at low tide, *Massachusetts* offers a spectacular dive and is home to myriad aquatic species. Somewhat the worse for wear, many of the ship's features still are easily recognized and the wreck often is visited by divers.

Florida's fifth Preserve, dedicated in 1994, is located off Pompano Beach on the east coast at the wreck of SS *Copenhagen*. A schooner-rigged screw steamship, *Copenhagen* was heading for Havana in 1900 with a load of coal when it ran aground at full speed on a shallow ledge. Although the cargo was saved, the vessel was a total loss and over the years became incorporated into the limestone reef. Bathed by the warm Gulf Stream, many varieties of tropical fish and invertebrates make their home on the wreck which is a popular shallow-water dive and snorkel site.

The sixth shipwreck to become a state Preserve was SS *Tarpon*, a merchant steamer that for thirty years plied the Gulf of Mexico between New Orleans, Louisiana, and Apalachicola, Florida. Heavily overloaded, *Tarpon* went down in a gale in 1937 with the loss of eighteen people. The *Tarpon* Preserve, dedicated in 1997, is located ten miles off the resort town of Panama City and is the deepest of Florida's Preserves at one hundred feet.

The creation of Florida's seventh Underwater Archaeological Preserve is an excellent example of the establishment process including the development of local partnerships. The vessel, a schooner-rigged racing yacht, was built in Germany in 1908 and was christened *Germania*; a nearly identical sister yacht was built for Kaiser Wilhelm II. *Germania* raced successfully in German and English regattas for several years until the British seized the yacht as a prize of war as World War I began. The vessel made its way to the United States where it was acquired by a former Assistant Secretary of the Navy who renamed it *Half Moon*. Sold south, the yacht finished its career in Miami, used as a floating saloon and fishing barge. Sunk in the 1930s off Key Biscayne near Miami, the chrome-nickel steel yacht's fine lines still are recognizable and it has become home to lobsters, corals, sponges, and enormous puffer fish. Partnerships with the University of Miami, local dive shops and yacht clubs, and the Biscayne Nature Center were formed and historical research was completed with assistance from maritime historians in England and Germany. The official Preserve Proposal was successfully presented to the people of Miami and the *Half Moon* Underwater Archaeological Preserve was dedicated in April of 2001.

## 3. ESTABLISHMENT, INTERPRETATION, AND MANAGEMENT

The method of establishing Florida's Underwater Archaeological Preserves has evolved considerably since the first designation more than a decade ago. Although all shipwrecks are unique and require different strategies to become a Florida Preserve, a useful pattern has evolved that ensures public participation and continuing local involvement with the project. For example, all potential Preserve sites are nominated by citizens and visitors via a mail-out form that also can be accessed at the Division's Preserve web site. The nominated site is visited by state archaeologists to determine if it meets the criteria (developed during the field school that selected *San Pedro*) for Preserve status: the shipwreck must lie within state waters, offer safe diving conditions, be accessible to the public, and have recognizable features and marine life. Research should document the ship's history and identity. These conditions met, the next step is to visit area businesses, chambers of commerce, museums, boating and fishing clubs, dive shops, and any other organization that might support a new Preserve and assist the project. Interested individuals, aided by state personnel, are encouraged to form a local Friends of the Shipwreck organization to promote and plan the Preserve. Past Friends groups have raised funds, conducted historical research, written books and articles, solicited donations and services from businesses, and in general enabled the Preserve to become a reality.

State archaeologists then survey and record the site to prepare a detailed site plan. Volunteers often perform this work and provide invaluable services and assistance. In order to teach volunteers field operations, a workshop to train sport divers in archaeological recording is held in cooperation with a local dive shop. Pool exercises and open water dives provide hands-on experience and graduates are invited to help map the shipwreck site.

Once the site plan and vessel history are complete, a public meeting is planned to present an official proposal for the new Preserve to area citizens and businesses and to address questions and concerns. The public meeting generally is held in conjunction with a local maritime history conference that includes regional experts and guest speakers. The proposal, which includes the site plan and ship history as well as economic and educational benefits of the Preserve, is distributed to area media such as newspapers, television, magazines, and radio. Public support generated through the proposal drives the effort and final steps for designating the site a State Underwater Archaeological Preserve are initiated.

Interpretation of the site takes several forms. A brochure presents the ship's history, how it came to be at its present location, a description of the underwater environment, an explanation of features, directions to find the site, and instructions for diving. Any special information is included as well, such as where to view photographs and artifacts in a shore-based exhibit (Figure 2). The Division's Underwater Archaeological Preserve Web page is updated with photos, directions to the site, the official site plan, and history of the new Preserve (http://dhr.dos.state.fl.us/bar/uap). A guide for divers is prepared showing the site plan; special features are labeled and a description of sea life is included. Laminated in plastic and equipped with a grommet for a lanyard, the guide can be used by divers to navigate around the site and identify parts of the ship. A local museum or other establishment generally hosts a shore-based exhibit including artifacts, pictures, and information. Finally, an opening ceremony dedicates the site with the placement of a plaque proclaiming the shipwreck a State Underwater Archaeological Preserve and Florida Heritage Site. Preserves also become part of Florida's Maritime Heritage Trail, which includes six themes for visitors to explore: shipwrecks, lighthouses, ports, coastal forts, communities, and environments (www.flheritage.com/maritime). Additionally, the information and history gathered are used to nominate the shipwreck to the National Register of Historic Places; to date, all of Florida's Preserves have been listed on the Register.

Management of Florida's Preserves is passive. A local dive shop or diving club generally adopts the Preserve and schedules regular trips to clean the site of debris and scrub growth off the plaque. State personnel visit each Preserve once a year to inspect the site, note any variation in its condition, and determine the extent, if any, of changes to the site. Mooring buoys are repaired, cleaned, or replaced as needed. Brochures are reprinted and distributed at every opportunity, such as water sports shows, mail-out packets, visitor information centers, and dive shops. Posters also have been useful for promoting the Preserve system.

**Figure 2.** A brochure for each Preserve is prepared for public distribution.

Within this framework, which has been tried and tested several times to date, there is much room for experimentation and variation. The Friends generally may be relied upon to answer site-specific questions. For example, the taking of fish, including tropical species, is discouraged around *Copenhagen* to protect its colorful aquarium-like setting. *Massachusetts*, however, for decades has been a favorite fishing spot because it is one of the only artificial reefs off Pensacola that can be located without electronics. The placement of mooring buoys also is determined by the Friends. Most of Florida's Preserves are outfitted with moorings to prevent anchor damage to the site and to provide convenient down-lines for divers. In the case of *Massachusetts*, not much could damage the three hundred-feet-long steel battleship and, in fact, boats could be damaged on the gun turrets if tied to a buoy during tidal change. Plaques differ from site to site as well. Bronze seems to hold up the best; imbedded in cement it makes an excellent permanent marker. At the *Hawkinsville* site the names of all the sponsors of the Preserve are included on the monument, while at *Massachusetts* the Winged Victory statue that once graced the forward turret was recreated for the plaque.

## 4. LESSONS LEARNED

Several lessons have been learned over ten years of creating Underwater Archaeological Preserves for Florida. The most important aspect is getting people involved--public participation is the key to Florida's Preserves. From the very beginning of a new Preserve project, the local community creates the impetus and the sustaining interest. Preserve nominations come from citizens and visitors, including teachers, charter boat captains, dive shop owners, and school children. The state program responds to a community request, provides technical assistance with details such as recording and research, and helps to direct and focus the Friends of the Shipwreck. Local people gain a sense of pride in their unique maritime heritage by becoming involved in historic preservation and promoting heritage tourism in their area. Businesses support Preserves because they draw tourist dollars and additional visitors. Preserve sites are protected from all types of disturbances by local divers and agencies.

The strength of Florida's Preserve system is the number of divers who visit these sites each year. With warm, clear water and diving opportunities ranging from oceans to springs to rivers, Florida is a top diving vacation destination. By combining education, recreation, and heritage tourism, underwater archaeological sites are yet another reason to visit Florida. Interpretation through brochures, guides, and exhibits encourages divers to learn rather than collect (Figure 3).

A weakness of Florida's Preserve program is the state's inability to monitor the number of visitors to each site. General statistics are available from the dive shops and charter boats that run trips to the sites, but comprehensive specifics are elusive. For example, many international tourists visit south Florida but there is no accurate method to quantify those who dive the *Copenhagen* Preserve. Is *Tarpon* visited by more local divers or mostly by tourists? Do the museum exhibits inspire people to dive the sites, or vice-versa? The next challenge is to determine a way to generate accurate Preserve visitation data.

There are several points of view to be considered in establishing underwater archaeological preserves, park, and trails. From a cultural resource management aspect, accelerated use often is not consistent with preservation. From a tourism point of view these types of attractions certainly draw diving visitors and are more "real Florida" than theme parks. From an

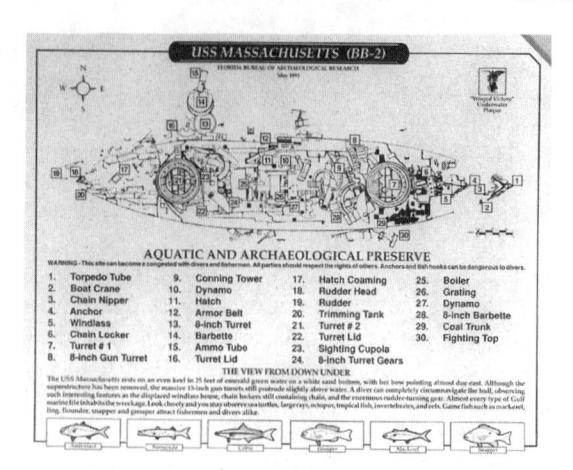

Figure 3. Laminated underwater guides direct divers around the Preserve sites.

archaeological perspective, Florida's citizens and visitors are educated about the real treasure of shipwrecks and, hopefully, will be more inclined to protect and conserve rather than collect and consume. From the sport diver's point of view these shipwrecks represent interesting dive locations with history and identity, as well as an opportunity to learn more about resources in the aquatic realm.

The intent of Florida's Underwater Archaeological Preserve system is to promote education through recreation while encouraging protection of submerged cultural resources. Florida has a large community of easily accessible shipwrecks located in its warm coastal waters, shallow rivers, and clear springs. These historical resources, like those on state-owned lands, belong to the people of Florida - state archaeologists merely have management responsibility. By encouraging citizens to adopt their local shipwreck Preserve, learn its history, and care for the site, a sense of stewardship is developed that helps to protect these resources from damage and exploitation. Public education and access builds the feeling of ownership and encourages local people to become guardians of their maritime heritage. Ultimately, shipwrecks with status as Underwater Archaeological Preserves are recorded for posterity, interpreted for the public, and protected for the future (Figure 4).

## 5. ISSUES AND CONCERNS

Florida's Preserve system is constantly growing and new nominations from all over the state are continually reviewed. Some are not suitable to become Preserves, such as wrecks outside state waters or those too deep for safe sport diving. Some wrecks are borderline and become the subject of much

# FLORIDA'S UNDERWATER ARCHAEOLOGICAL PRESERVES 103

discussion and debate. For example, a flat-bottomed Civil War-era steamboat in a spring run has been nominated--it is certainly historic and,

**Figure 4.** The Preserve system encourages divers to visit and learn about Florida's historic shipwrecks.

because it was the subject of a master's thesis, its history is known. The water is crystal clear and it is even in a state park, but all that is left are a few bottom frames barely protruding above the sand and it is not visually interesting. What is the answer for this wreck? If it is made a Preserve more people will visit it and learn of its role in riverine warfare; however, interested but ill-informed divers might fan away the thin protective layer of sand that keeps the remaining timbers from being eroded. In this case, making this site a Preserve might not be the wisest use of the resource. Vessels sunk intentionally as artificial reefs also are questionable for Preserve status. They may not be "natural" shipwrecks but some of them have fascinating backgrounds and may be considered valuable historical resources as well as make excellent Preserves.

The question of "enhancing" a site for divers is open for debate as well. The sites of *Urca de Lima* and *San Pedro*, for example, were discovered by treasure hunters who removed the cannons and anchors. The addition of cement replica cannons to these Preserves gives visitors a better idea of how the wreck looked before being salvaged and provides a more interesting experience for divers. Now well-covered with marine growth the replica guns appear almost as historic as the real things. But is it archaeologically correct to enhance sites?

## 6. CONCLUSION

Nominations of shipwrecks to Florida's Preserve system are often received and, at any given time, at least one site is being established. A steamship wreck in St. Augustine is being researched and mapped by high school students as a class project under the direction of archaeologists. This wreck's identity still needs to be determined but it likely will make an excellent Preserve candidate. A not-for-profit avocational archaeology group in south Florida mapped and nominated the remains of a Norwegian barque, called *Lofthus*, wrecked off Boynton Beach, and a dive shop in Bradenton Beach nominated the wreck of *Regina*, a 1940s sugar tanker, which will be the first Preserve on Florida's west coast. Perhaps the most distinctive idea for a new Preserve is a prehistoric site in one of Florida's springs. To date, only large, highly visible shipwrecks have become Preserves, but Florida has numerous early Native American sites, often associated with fossils of the megafauna they hunted. A proposal has been made to recreate one of these sites using casts of fossils and replica stone tools placed in an accessible clear-water spring for snorkeling and glass-bottom boat viewing. When dedicated, "Pleistocene Park" will become a unique prehistoric Underwater Archaeological Preserve.

With one of the largest preserve programs in the world, the state of Florida is constantly seeking to expand and improve its system. Eventually, state archaeologists hope the state will be ringed with dozens of Underwater Archeological Preserves representing all aspects and ages of Florida's maritime heritage.

## FURTHER READING

Bane, M., 1992, USS Massachusetts, *Rodale's Scuba Diving* December:13-14.
Florida Bureau of Archaeological Research, 2001, Tallahassee; http://dhr.dos.state.fl.us/bar/uap or www.flheritage.com/preserves
Florida Bureau of Archaeological Research, 2000, Tallahassee; www.flheritage.com/maritime
Miller, J.J., 1989, Managing Florida's historic shipwrecks, *Underwater Archaeology Proceedings* 1989:53-55.
Reeves, L., 2001, Historic Florida wrecks, *Rodale's Scuba Diving* 10(2):42-47.
Smith, R.C., 1991, Florida's underwater archaeological preserves, *Underwater Archaeology Proceedings* 1991:43-46.

CHAPTER 9

# BENEATH PICTURED ROCKS

John R. Halsey and Peter Lindquist*

## 1. INTRODUCTION

The Alger Great Lakes State Bottomland Preserve was one of the first two preserves designated under Michigan's Public Act 184 of 1980. There are now eleven preserves. The Alger Preserve lies in Lake Superior offshore from some of the Upper Peninsula of Michigan's most spectacular natural scenery: the forests, sandstone cliffs, and enormous sand dunes of Hiawatha National Forest and Pictured Rocks National Lakeshore (Figure 1), a premier tourist attraction area. Containing nearly two dozen known shipwrecks, the Alger Preserve offers some of the best shipwreck diving in the Great Lakes due to its cold, clear water. Unfortunately, that beautiful water may still be ice in May and the diving season is essentially over by Labor Day. This chapter examines how a local entrepreneur, co-author Peter Lindquist, expanded his business from offering only dive charters to coordinating dive charters and glass-bottom boat tours that in 1998 allowed thirteen thousand non-divers to get a close-up view of some of these wrecks, as well as how the local community now views these heretofore largely inaccessible tourist attractions. Additionally, significant accomplishments at other Michigan preserves will be discussed, such as the placement of the state's first underwater historical marker on the tug *Sport* (1873-1920) by the Sanilac Shores Underwater Preserve (Peters and Ashlee, 1992; Stayer and Stayer, 1995:73-80) and the basic training course in underwater archaeological techniques offered through the Straits of Mackinac Preserve (Harrington, 1990).

---

*John R. Halsey, Office of the State Archaeologist, Michigan Historical Center, Lansing, Michigan 48918. Peter Lindquist, Shipwreck Tours, Inc., 1204 Commercial Street, Munising, Michigan 49862.

**Figure 1.** Spectacular sandstone cliffs and Lake Superior's cold, clear water make Pictured Rocks National Lakeshore one of the premier scenic attractions in the upper Midwest.

## 2. MICHIGAN'S GREAT LAKES STATE BOTTOMLAND PRESERVES

The Great Lakes of midcontinental North America are the largest system of connected freshwater lakes in the world (Sommers, 1977:43) containing one-quarter of the planet's fresh water (National Geographic Society, 1978:145). Michigan has title to thirty-eight thousand five hundred and four square miles of bottomland lying beneath Lakes Superior, Michigan, Huron, Erie, and St. Clair, or roughly forty percent of the estimated ninety-five thousand square miles taken up by all of the Great Lakes including Lake Ontario. Michigan's bottomland area *alone* is larger than the land area of Hungary or Portugal and thirteen of the United States. Upon Michigan's bottomlands rest more than thirteen hundred shipwrecks, the first, LaSalle's *Griffon*, lost in 1679.

Throughout the 1960s and 1970s, the State of Michigan, through its Department of Natural Resources (DNR), attempted a variety of initiatives to protect these wrecks or at least to regulate the wholesale removal of shipwreck artifacts that was taking place (Halsey, 1985). Most of these initiatives were actively opposed or ignored by many sport divers. By the end of the 1970s, however, even the most hard-core collectors admitted that wrecks were being destroyed at a rate that threatened the future of recreational diving in Michigan waters. Finally, the Michigan legislature passed Public Law 184 of 1980. This act established a formal process for the salvaging of bottomland materials by permits jointly administered by the Department of State (DOS) and the Department of Natural Resources. This act also mandated that the DNR establish "Great Lakes State Bottomland Preserves." These preserves could be based on recreational and/or historical values and were limited to not more than five percent of Michigan's total bottomland area or about one thousand nine hundred and twenty five square miles, an area about the size of Delaware.

Over the next eight years it became obvious that there were deficiencies in this law and an amended law was passed as Public Act 452 of 1988 (Halsey, 1989, 1990). The new law specifically prohibited all forms of mechanical or other assistance in recovering loose artifacts from the bottom. The permit application process for the DNR and the DOS was clarified and additional responsibilities were laid on the permit holder, who was required to submit a specific removal plan prior to commencement of salvage, was prohibited or limited in the amount of discharge of possible pollutants, and was prohibited from injuring, harming, or damaging a site or property not authorized for removal during and after salvage operations. The law considerably toughened the penalty phase making it a felony to recover or destroy abandoned property with a fair market value of $100 or more, and punishable by imprisonment for not more than two years or by a fine of not more than $5,000, or both. The law also provided for the confiscation, condemnation, and sale of watercraft, mechanical or other assistance, scuba gear, sonar equipment, motor vehicles, or any other apparatus used in violation of the act. The amount of bottomland potentially available for preserve was raised from five percent to ten percent, or three thousand eight hundred and fifty square miles, an area about the size of Puerto Rico.

There had long been concerns about the liability for injuries or death for divers on state-owned wrecks. To address this matter, the law adapted language that had been used successfully by ski resort operators to protect themselves from personal injury suits specifying that:

> Each person who participates in the sport of scuba diving on the Great Lakes accepts the dangers which adhere in that sport insofar as the dangers are obvious and necessary. Those dangers include, but are not limited to, injuries which can result from entanglements in sunken watercraft or aircraft; the condition of sunken watercraft or aircraft; the location of sunken watercraft or aircraft; the failure of the state to fund staff or programs at bottomland preserves; and the depth of the objects and bottomlands within preserves.

Important for the discussion here, the law also made it legal to intentionally sink not more than one "vessel associated with Great Lakes maritime history" within each preserve, but no state funds were to be expended to purchase, transport, or sink the vessel. This last statement continued the Michigan legislature's position of providing no funding for enforcement, administration, or interpretation in the preserves. In effect, the law was saying, "Whatever is going to happen in a preserve will depend upon private initiative and funding," and so it came to be. The topic of intentional sinking will be explored later.

## 3. PARKS AND PRESERVES: WHAT'S THE DIFFERENCE?

From the very beginning of the State of Michigan's entry into shipwreck legislation and management, there has been little distinction made between the terms "underwater parks" and "bottomland preserves" by the public or the communications media. The source of the confusion is old and deep-seated. Initial proposals (e.g. Warner, 1974) envisioned "parks" with organized water-based recreational activities such as tour boats, sport diving and service facilities, interpretive programs (both on land and below water), and programs of environmental and historical research and education. Such a park existed at that time in nascent form and was well-known to park planners and Great Lakes divers--Ontario's Fathom Five Provincial Park located at the northern tip of the Bruce Peninsula in Lake Huron (McClellan, 1985).

Preserves, on the other hand, carry no direct implication or necessary expectation of physical facilities. They are the underwater equivalents of land-based natural or wilderness areas, bounded by imaginary lines drawn on the water according to certain coordinates and encompassing a certain number of square miles. There was also the expectation that there would be little in the way of regulations.

## 4. ALGER GREAT LAKES STATE BOTTOMLAND PRESERVE

The Alger Preserve came into being in June of 1981, and was broadly supported by such organizations as the local chamber of commerce, historical society, Rotary Club, the City of Munising, and the Alger County Sheriff. The preserve covers two hundred ninety three square kilometers (one hundred and thirteen square miles) with its western boundary at Au Train Point and its eastern boundary at Au Sable Point, and extends lakeward (north) to the 45.72 meters (one hundred and fifty feet) depth contour. The earliest preserve promotional brochure listed only thirteen "dive sites": seven shipwrecks locations, four submerged rock formations and caves, one former dock location, and one weed bed with fish. Major problems with the preserve, from a dive-access viewpoint, were its length (approximately sixty four kilometers, or forty miles), the great distances between wrecks, and the exposed nature of the coast with no refuge for dive boats if the weather deteriorated on the world's largest freshwater lake. Even before the official designation of the preserve, some local promoters were interested in the deliberate placement of one or more vessels to offer additional dive attractions in a sheltered area, i.e., a bad weather dive site. The deliberate sinking of a vessel, or "salting" as it was commonly known, was a topic much discussed throughout the early 1980s with the local divers (but not necessarily the local population) in favor of it, and state agencies consistently opposed on philosophical and practical (i.e., liability) grounds.

## 5. ACTIVITIES OF THE ALGER UNDERWATER PRESERVE COMMITTEE

Alger has always been one of the most active of Michigan's preserves. One of the early actions of the Alger committee was to conduct a survey of divers who visited the preserve in the 1985 diving season to gauge their impact on the local economy. The sample of on hundred and thirty three of an estimated six thousand divers (and an unknown number of non-diving companions) yielded an estimate of well over $2 million being spent in Alger County by divers (Alger Underwater Preserve Committee, Inc., 1985)!

Since the bedrock in Alger County is sandstone, loose sand on the bottom periodically covers some wrecks partially or completely. In 1988, the preserve committee acquired funding to remove more than 531.5 cubic meters (seven hundred cubic yards) of sand that accumulated on one of the preserve's most important attractions, the wooden bulk freighter *Smith Moore* (1880-1889), resting in 27.4 meters (ninety feet) of water. The dredging was accomplished successfully, but due to the ultimate futility of trying to dictate to Lake Superior where it can and cannot move sand, it has not been attempted again.

*Smith Moore* had been a dive destination since scuba diving began in the Great Lakes and almost every loose artifact, regardless of size, had been removed. A chance meeting of two cousins, however, led to the discovery of the location of two coal grates from the wreck and their replacement in their original locations on the vessel (Laraway, 1994).

Also in 1988, the National Park Service, assisted by local preserve divers, undertook a major inventory of the submerged cultural resources offshore from Pictured Rocks National Lakeshore. This project documented twenty three wrecks, tripling the number of wrecks known at the time of preserve designation and improving the preserve's cachet as a dive destination. This report provided a regional maritime historical context and a developmental sequence of commercial ships on Lake Superior. Individual vessel histories and wreck events are provided along with site descriptions and analyses, shipwreck plans, and historic photographs (Labadie, 1989). Although the survey was done under the auspices of the National Park Service, the wrecks were the property of the State of Michigan because the bottomlands on which they lay had not been ceded to the federal government as was the case when Isle Royale National Park was created.

One of the highlight dives in the Alger Preserve is the *Bermuda* (1860-1870), a marvelously intact forty three meter (one hundred and forty one feet) canal schooner lying on the flat, sandy bottom of Grand Island's Murray Bay in only 10.7 meters (thirty five feet) of water with only about three meters (ten feet) of water to the deck (Figure 2). Due to the excellent condition, shallow depth, water clarity, and schools of friendly (i.e., diver-fed) fish, it is one of the most visited wrecks in the Great Lakes (Harrington, 1998:72; Kohl, 1998:373-377). Despite its popularity, divers would often spend only thirty minutes on the wreck declaring that they had seen it all. To inform divers of the numerous archaeological and natural resource values of the wreck, the preserve committee contracted with Maritime Research Associates, Inc. to create the first underwater interpretive trail on the United States side of the Great Lakes. Funded by the Michigan Department of Natural Resource's Coastal Zone Management Program, the trail includes seventeen stops identified by colorful laminated numbers, but unobtrusively placed so as not to interfere with underwater photography. Local dive charter operators provide free use of underwater slates that explain the features at the stop. The interested diver can learn about ship construction, cargoes and their importance in the development of the Midwest, the varieties of fish found on the wreck, and even tiny freshwater sponges. Divers responded well to the trail and instead of spending just thirty minutes, made *Bermuda* a full dive with some returning to complete or repeat the trail (Anonymous, 1993).

As noted above, Public Act 452 of 1988 allowed the intentional sinking of one vessel per preserve. What the law did not say was just how difficult this would be. To discover what was really required, Michigan state officials commissioned a study report (Harrington, 1993). A deliberate sinking requires permission from a variety of state and federal agencies with a range of concerns: placement, location, and depth, but most of all, cleanliness. Every candidate

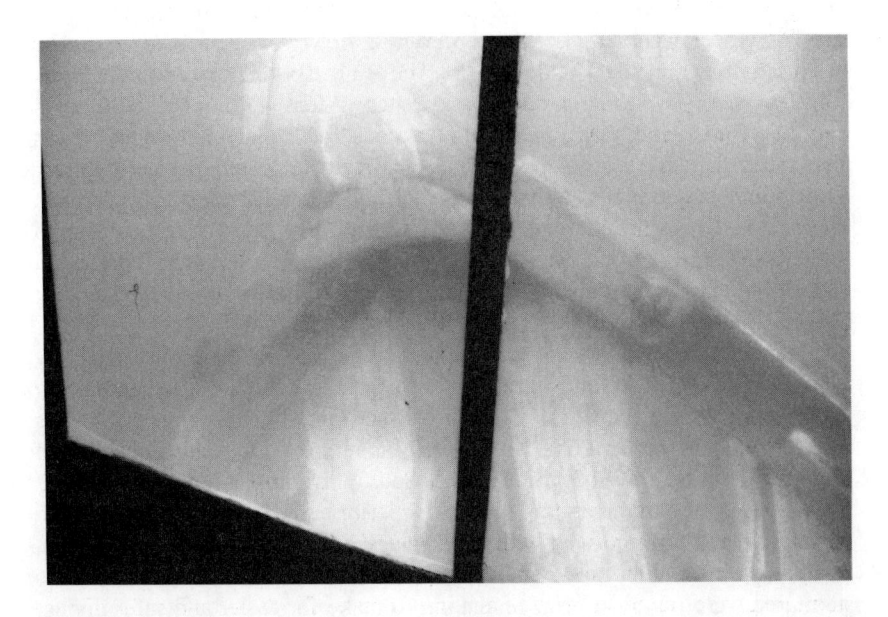

**Figure 2.** The bow of the schooner *Bermuda* lies only twelve feet below the surface of Grand Island's Murray Bay.

vessel would need to have any asbestos, PCBs, fuel oil, lubricants, etc., removed and legally disposed of, and engines, bilges, etc., disassembled (if necessary) and thoroughly cleaned. Early dreams of sinking an obsolete ore carrier vanished in the reality of the effort required to clean a 213.3 meter (seven hundred foot) vessel from stem to stern using only voluntary labor, assuming a place to dock it could be found while the years of cleaning took place. A candidate vessel was finally identified in the obsolete 21.6 meter (seventy one foot) tug *Steven M. Selvick* (1915-1996).

In a strictly technical sense, *Selvick* was not the first vessel to be intentionally placed on the bottom. The USCG cutter *Mesquite* ran aground in 3.6 meters (twelve feet) of water at Lake Superior's Keweenaw Point on

December 4, 1989; damages suffered during the wrecking incident and a winter spent on the rocks made *Mesquite* a total loss. Gross cleaning such as removal of diesel fuel was done at the time of the grounding. Eventually ownership of the wreck was transferred to the State of Michigan and the decommissioned remains of *Mesquite*, minus its upper works, were lifted, moved, and placed in 30.48 meters (one hundred plus feet) of water in Keystone Bay, a few kilometers southwest of its grounding point (Stonehouse, 1991). In effect, the vessel had already sunk and it was just a question of moving it to another place on the bottom. *Mesquite* has since become a major attraction in the Keweenaw Great Lakes State Bottomland Preserve.

The vessel eventually known as *Steven M. Selvick*, began its career as the steam tug *Lorain* in Cleveland in 1915. The tug had a long career on the Great Lakes, primarily working on construction sites. After working in the Sturgeon Bay area for several years, *Selvick* lay at dock for a year after which it was discovered that the vessel's rusting riveted steel hull could not be repaired. After some negotiations, *Selvick* was donated to the preserve by Selvick Marine and Towing of Sturgeon Bay, Wisconsin. In 1994, Pete Lindquist and Mike Kohut arranged and oversaw the towing of *Selvick* from Sturgeon Bay on Lake Michigan to Munising on Lake Superior (Harrington, 1998:80-81; Lindquist, 1995).

Nearly two years were required to get *Selvick* adequately cleaned by volunteers and to raise funds through the sale of caps and T-shirts announcing "I Helped Sink the Steven M. Selvick." Over the winter, volunteer cleaners walked to an iced-in *Selvick*. On June 1,1996, approved by state and Corps of Engineer permits, *Steven M. Selvick*, flooded by fire hoses, quickly sank 18.3 meters (sixty feet) to the bottom of Lake Superior east of Trout Point on Grand Island. Today, sport divers will find *Selvick* lying on its port side and can easily inspect the pilot house and the engine room. Several deck plates in the stern area were removed prior to sinking to make for easier and safer diving. Doors have been permanently blocked open for the same reason. The rudder, detached during the sinking, lies nearby.

## 6. FROM DIVERS TO GLASS-BOTTOM BOATS

In 1980, Pete Lindquist started his own dive charter service in Munising after working several years with longtime local charter operator and diver, Tom Bathey. Over the years, it became apparent to Lindquist that there was a broad public interest in shipwrecks, beyond the obvious interest held by scuba divers. He wondered how non-divers could view shipwrecks and get something of the thrill that divers experience and discussed the situation with Bathey. Bathey thought of creating a boat tour for non-divers that would use an experienced diver with a television camera so that viewers topside could watch television screens as the diver explored the shipwreck below. Lindquist considered this option, but decided that it would be too costly and the customers would only get to see one shipwreck and hear one story. There had to be a better way.

Lindquist realized that many of the wrecks in the immediate Munising area were visible over the side of a boat. Remembering the flocks of tourists who gathered at the city park on the waterfront every Fourth of July, he considered running an Independence Day charter for non-divers to see one of the wrecks in that area. The problem with this idea was that his boat could only hold six passengers per trip, which would never be profitable.

He continued to mull the problems and possibilities of getting non-divers to shipwrecks. One day, he walked out on his dock and noticed *Divemaster*, a large dive charter vessel licensed to carry eighteen passengers, but hardly ever used. The owner lived in Chicago and *Divemaster* was badly in need of maintenance. Lindquist called *Divemaster*'s owner and struck a deal whereby Lindquist offered to maintain the boat in exchange for its use and payment of $2.50 on each $14.00 individual ticket sold. Lindquist could now advertise a tour that could carry up to eighteen passengers and Shipwreck Tours, Inc. was born.

In August, 1994, the first tours began. Brochures were printed and distributed locally and across the Upper Peninsula advertising what was ingenuously called an "Almost Glass-Bottom Boat Tour." The tour, then as now, lasted about two hours and showed passengers three shipwrecks along with above-water historic sites along Munising Bay (Figure 3). On these early tours passengers simply looked over the side of the boat to view the underwater wrecks, yet they loved it! The half-season in 1994 produced two hundred and fifty seven passengers. Feedback from the passengers was so positive that "Captain Pete" decided to buy *Divemaster*.

**Figure 3.** Billboards outside Munising, Michigan, announce the presence of an exciting historical attraction.

The following year, Lindquist purchased *Divemaster* and received permits from the U. S. Coast Guard to install a "through-hull glass viewing area." As there were no other vessels of this type on the Great Lakes, he had to work closely with Coast Guard engineers to create a design that would pass inspection. By June of 1995, *Divemaster* became the first "glass-bottom boat" to carry passengers in U.S. Great Lakes waters. Remodeling allowed seating for thirty six and the 1995 season produced one thousand and sixty seven passengers.

Spring of 1996 brought more changes. With permits from the Coast Guard, Lindquist enlarged the viewing area from two feet by six feet to four feet by nine feet, thereby tripling the viewing area of his previous design. The number of passengers that year also more than tripled to three thousand nine hundred, a number Lindquist thought probably was the limit *Divemaster* could handle.

Over the winter of 1996-1997, Lindquist purchased *Miss Munising*, a sixty feet-long steel-hulled vessel from Pictured Rocks Cruises, Inc., a company that had offered close-up views of the Pictured Rocks since 1950. He went back to the Coast Guard to obtain permits for two new viewing areas, each measuring four feet by ten feet, more than doubling the viewing area on *Divemaster*. Able to carry up to one hundred passengers at a time, *Miss Munising* accommodated seven thousand nine hundred passengers in its first season and was such a success that *Divemaster* was retired.

In the winter of 1997-98, Lindquist began construction of a new gift shop and ticket office to replace the tiny dive shop that had previously housed both operations. The building was finished and open for business in June 1998. Profiting by word of mouth and good weather, *Miss Munising* carried over thirteen thousand passengers that year. On a typical tour, visitors are given capsule histories of the life and death of each ship and what they are seeing as *Miss Munising* hovers, sometimes only a few feet, above the wreck. On a fully-booked tour, the presentations must be given twice, once for the lower-deck passengers and again for the upper-deck passengers who change places with those on the lower deck. Plans are being made to purchase additional vessels.

Over this time span Lindquist has continued to offer dive charters and to coordinate with individual divers. The *Bermuda* is always the first stop on the shipwreck tour. Before leaving the dock, a security call on the radio alerts divers of the probable arrival time. There is also a sign posted on the mooring buoy asking divers to avoid diving at the times of the tour. If a dive is interrupted, divers are asked to come up and stay on the surface while *Miss Munising* drifts over the wreck. In exchange, the divers get a free air fill. Cooperation with the request is the norm and divers are saluted with a thank you on the loudspeaker and a group wave from the boat.

Because they are exploiting different "resource niches," cooperative relations and cross promotion with the much larger and well-established Pictured Rocks Cruises has benefited both operations. Spring outfitting at the same location brings both operations together and discussions of common problems lead to improvements such as rubber mounts to quiet engine noise.

The shipwreck tour has brought shipwrecks into the discussions of the local community. In restaurants after a tour, visitors are excited about what they have seen and waitresses often have to field questions about which tour, Pictured Rocks or shipwrecks, is the "best." Local service clubs have taken the tour as part of their programs and are strong supporters. The shipwreck tour is now the second largest private tourist draw in the area behind Pictured Rocks Cruises.

## 7. CONCLUSION

Developments at the Alger Great Lakes State Bottomlands Preserve have increased the interpretation, protection, and availability of shipwrecks to sport divers and to the general public in ways that begin to approach the dreams of early park planners. However, it is not a model that can easily be superimposed on other preserves. Blessed with shallow wrecks, clear water, and an abundant supply of tourists drawn by the region's scenic attractions, glass-bottom boat tours work here, but probably would not at other preserves. The Alger Preserve has been fortunate to find a cooperative partner in the adjacent Pictured Rocks National Lakeshore which provides the visitor center/museum function otherwise lacking in Munising. Perhaps, as is evident to the authors, the success is due to the mutual respect that has developed among entrepreneurs, state administrators, and federal officials over more than two decades of unbroken cooperation that has allowed Alger to blossom with the implicit understanding that it is acceptable to make a profit from these shipwreck resources as long as their long-term survival and better understanding is everyone's primary goal.

# REFERENCES

Anonymous, 1993, Underwater trail enhances shipwreck diving at Alger Underwater Preserve, *Michigan Underwater Preserve Council Newsletter* Winter:1, 4.

Alger Underwater Preserve Committee, Inc., 1985, *1985 Alger Underwater Preserve Diver Information Survey Results, Expenditures, and Secondary Economic Impacts*, Munising, Michigan.

Halsey, J., 1990, *Beneath the Inland Seas: Michigan's Underwater Archaeological Heritage*, Bureau of History, Michigan Department of State, Lansing, Michigan.

Halsey, J., 1989, Nine years before the mast: Shipwreck management in Michigan since 1980, in: *Underwater Archaeology Proceedings from the Society for Historical Archaeology Conference*, J. Barto Arnold III, ed., Society for Historical Archaeology, Baltimore, pp. 43-48.

Halsey, J., 1985, Michigan's Great Lakes bottomland preserves, in: *Marine Parks & Conservation: Challenge and Promise* Vol. 2, Jon Lien and Robert Graham, eds., National and Provincial Parks Association of Canada, Toronto, pp. 65-76.

Harrington, S., 1998, *Divers Guide to Michigan*, Maritime Press Inc., Grand Rapids, Michigan.

Harrington, S., 1993, *Intentional Vessel Sinking Guidelines: Final Report*, Maritime Research Associates, St. Ignace, Michigan.

Harrington, S., ed., 1990, *Diving into St. Ignace Past: An Underwater Investigation of East Moran Bay*, Maritime Press, Mason, Michigan.

Kohl, C., 1998, *The 100 Best Great Lakes Shipwrecks, Volume II: Lake Michigan, Lake Superior*, Seawolf Communications, Inc., West Chicago, Illinois.

Labadie, C. P., 1989, *Submerged Cultural Resources Study: Pictured Rocks National Lakeshore*, Southwest Cultural Resources Center Professional Papers No. 22, Santa Fe, New Mexico.

Laraway, L., 1994, Home at last, *Dive Munising News*, Edition 1, pp. 1.

Lindquist, P., 1995, Steven M. Selvick, *Dive Munising News*, Edition 1, pp. 1, 4.

McClellan, S., 1985, Fathom Five Provincial Park: Working example of an underwater park, in: *Marine Parks & Conservation: Challenge and Promise* Vol. 2, Jon Lien and Robert Graham, eds., National and Provincial Parks Association of Canada, Toronto, pp. 173-177.

National Geographic Society, 1978, *National Geographic Picture Atlas of Our Fifty States*, National Geographic Society, Washington, D. C.

Peters, S., and Ashlee, L., 1992, Working for a living, *Michigan History Magazine* 76(6):47-51.

Sommers, L., ed., 1977, *Atlas of Michigan*, Michigan State University Press, East Lansing, Michigan.

Stayer, P. and J. Stayer, 1995, *Shipwrecks of Sanilac*, Out of the Blue Productions, Lexington, Michigan.

Stonehouse, F., 1991, *Shipwreck of the Mesquite: Death of a United States Coast Guard Cutter*, Lake Superior Port Cities Inc., Duluth, Minnesota.

Warner, Thomas, 1974, *Proposed Thunder Bay Underwater Historical Park*, Department of Park and Recreation Resources, Michigan State University, East Lansing, Michigan.

# PART III: TRAILS

Part III concerns the grouping of individual maritime archaeological sites into themed trails that lead visitors from site to site. Some trails can be seen in a day, while others may require a number of visits to see all the sites. The four chapters in this section discuss and review the processes used to construct and maintain trails. The first two chapters are devoted to the shipwreck trail system in Australia; the final chapters describe trails in the United States.

Tim Smith provides a review of the static nature of the Australian shipwreck trail system and describes the unfortunate neglect of existing trails as submerged cultural resource managers focus on creating additional trails. Smith offers reasons for the neglect such as legislation initiatives to create trails and lack of funding and personnel. Additionally, states and museums tend to create trails without the broad community support necessary for continued success. Smith suggests that submerged cultural resource managers look to the land and use as a model a successful terrestrial trail that relies heavily on community support to maintain the education and preservation mission.

Cassandra Philippou and Mark Staniforth evaluate the state of Australian shipwreck trails. The authors consider whether the trails have succeeded in providing visitors with thought-provoking and rewarding visits to maritime resources. They assess several state shipwreck trail programs and their interpretive materials and conclude with an analysis of the respective programs. The authors propose that future directions for Australia's shipwreck trail system should be devoted to providing better and more cohesive presentations of maritime resources to the public.

The Florida Keys National Marine Sanctuary Shipwreck Trail is presented by Bruce Terrell. The trail is described as a means to promote access to shipwrecks in the Sanctuary and to mitigate human impact on coral reefs, which are the main attraction for sport divers in the Keys. The author relates the forging of partnerships among federal agencies, state and local government, and private organizations to implement the trail. Terrell concludes with ideas for future directions for the trail and the need for continued active management of the resources.

The last chapter by Jim Spirek and Lynn Harris narrates the creation of two trails near Charleston, South Carolina, that focus on submerged cultural resources in a tidal riverine environment. Sites along the river trails are accessible by recreational paddlers and sport divers and provide visitors with access to cultural as well as natural resources. The authors describe the impetus for creating the trails and relate the interpretation and infrastructure necessary to make the sites accessible to the public.

CHAPTER 10

# SHIPWRECK TRAILS: PUBLIC OWNERSHIP OF A UNIQUE RESOURCE?

## An Australian perspective

Tim Smith[*]

### 1. INTRODUCTION

The last major review of the Australian Commonwealth Historic Shipwrecks Program (CHSP) was undertaken in 1985 (Kenderdine, 1985). A major focus of that plan was the targeting of ways of further promoting Australia's shipwreck heritage to the public. Since that time, little appears to have been achieved at a national level, while each component state-based maritime archaeology program continues with its own program of site assessment, protection, and, when time and money permits, promotion of local heritage sites.

In the mid-1990s, Dr. Michael McCarthy of the Western Australian Maritime Museum lamented the then-perceived failure of practitioners to pay due attention to the *people* involved with the material remains through published works and debates (McCarthy, 1998). This was a criticism of the traditional background of the national program that appeared based on descriptive study of material artifacts (particularly in light of major excavation projects at the time). His theme was that much of the professional study of shipwrecks and related sites had become very site specific and remains oriented. Part of this was seen to result from the focus of state-based agencies responsible for historic shipwreck management on stocktaking the shipwreck

---

[*] Tim Smith, Underwater Heritage Program, New South Wales Heritage Office, Locked Bag 5020, 2-10 Wentworth Street, Level 11, Parramatta, New South Wales 2124, Australia.

resource and from the demands of implementing the current legislative controls. McCarthy identified the need for a more anthropological approach to future study of shipwreck remains which would get the people back onto the wrecks.

This theme, noted in the 1995 Research Plan, identified the need of the Commonwealth Historic Shipwrecks Program to develop research initiatives to take a wider view of the place of historic shipwrecks in Australian society. It was felt that this would lead to a "commitment to public education" and an increase in awareness and appreciation of historic shipwreck sites (Kenderdine, 1995).

The reporting team identified constraints in the Australian maritime archaeology scene. Principle amongst these was the disparity between state Maritime Archaeology Programs, run through either maritime museums or cultural resource management "planning" type agencies. The former were seen to be historically better founded for interpretative initiatives with their research base and public display focus, while the strength of cultural resource based agencies was noted with the conduct of their administrative responsibilities implementing heritage legislation and preliminary site surveys for management purposes.

This traditional picture is demonstrated by the first attempts at developing large-scale public education projects in Australia. The earliest shipwreck trails were initiated by maritime museums, the first by the Western Australian Maritime Museum at Rottnest Island, near Perth, since 1981. This first major educational initiative evolved some eight years after state-based protective legislation had come into force and more than a decade after maritime archaeology began to be practiced in that state. The project was a massive leap forward, however in a climate where cultural heritage tourism was an unknown entity, and it captured many people's imaginations. The museum's Wreck Access and Interpretation Program has continued to develop and diversify since that time (McCarthy and Garratt, 1998). In time, the cultural research management agencies also developed a strong lead role in public education initiatives and in the dispersal of information to the public at a state level.

The 1995 Research Plan had suggested as one of its major recommendations the establishment of a *National Shipwrecks Interpretation Plan* to guide future educational initiatives. It was suggested that the Commonwealth Government establish a consultantcy group to guide this plan from the 1995-96 financial year. Over six years later there has been little movement, with the annual Commonwealth grant to the state-based agencies reduced if anything over this period. A submission for funding a national shipwreck trail, partly in an attempt to generate more conformity in historic shipwreck trail design and broader coverage, was not forthcoming (personal communication, Bill Jeffery, 2001).

Another attempt to kick-start a complementary interpretative project in 2001, the national documentation and promotion of Australia's Federation Period shipwrecks sites (i.e., post-1900) under a special Government Centenary of Federation grants scheme, was also unsuccessful. Does this signal the hiatus of such projects nationally? The current history of heritage funding endeavors does not seem to bode well. The risk is that the development of a nationally focused shipwreck interpretation program may flounder for another five years awaiting favorable economic timing.

There is a continued need, however, to put in place more interpretation and promotion of the heritage we have. This is a reflection of the massive growth in information technology currently available through venues such as the Internet and mass media generally. People are hungry for quick, ready information and for innovative learning experiences. This is not to underestimate the many successes to date in Australia at a local and regional level. There is, however, still a long way to go in making knowledge more accessible and Australia's significant maritime heritage places better understood.

Learning and understanding is a fundamental part in fostering sound heritage conservation values. In this it supports one of the key objectives of the Commonwealth Historic Shipwrecks Program, the "gaining of an informed public for heritage conservation."

## 2. REVIEW OF LARGE-SCALE SHIPWRECK INTERPRETATION PROJECTS IN AUSTRALIA

Strachan in 1995 reviewed the then-current state of shipwreck heritage trails in Australia. Her report provided a background to trail development and implementation and a critique of potential downfalls. A major finding was the lack of on-going promotion of a trail once it was established. This was seen to reflect the energy put into the initial construction, the fact that government and museum institutions are not necessarily geared toward the tourism and marketing sphere, and the lack of a national plan or comprehensive design concept.

As noted above, the first trail attempts were carried out in Western Australia, the Rottnest Island shipwreck resource being showcased by both above ground and underwater diver signage (McCarthy, 1983). Most of the early trails were linked around a limited geographical land-based walking trail and/or underwater diving trail. The concept was tied together through maps and illustrative brochures--a format that has remained virtually unchanged in all subsequent Australian trail designs. While such projects have been partially successful in heralding the presence of underwater heritage sites to the general public and by promoting the need for careful scientific study, conservation, protection, and care of the fragile remains, they have also been limited by the constraints of their very genesis. In many ways, the existing Australian shipwreck trails (some forty in 2001, not including stand-alone interpretative plinths or signs) remain static and lacking in vision. There appears little local "ownership" of the established trails, many of which have languished because of later priorities and goals. They are in many ways under-utilized as a learning resource and are requiring of extensive input in terms of maintenance, advertising, and promotion. McCarthy noted from the Western Australian experience that trails have been "gradually implemented in an ad hoc fashion, subject to expressions of institutional or regional interest, and the provision of material, logistical, and monetary support from that institution or region" (McCarthy and Garratt, 1998:128).

When reviewing the national picture, of some sixty-five hundred known historic shipwreck losses in Australian waters, approximately five hundred sites, or under 8% of the national whole, have been linked by public access trails (see also Strachan, 1995). Of these, only five states (Western Australia, South Australia, Victoria, Tasmania, and New South Wales) have established trails of some sort. Only those in New South Wales have been totally driven by local communities; the others were initiated (albeit with associated local government, business, and community assistance) by the local state agency responsible for the implementation of the Historic Shipwrecks Program. Responsibility for upkeep and development is often retained by these organizations. Strachan observed that this was a possible factor in the lack of continued successes with trail development.

## 3. MEASURING THE SUCCESS OF TRAIL ESTABLISHMENT

One of the underlying principles of the Commonwealth Historic Shipwrecks Program has been in the belief that the nation's underwater heritage is a resource that should be accessible to all, so long as it is respected and maintained for future generation to enjoy. Thus the majority of the country's shipwreck sites have no visitation restrictions placed upon them (apart from a limited number with Protected Zones under the Commonwealth Historic Shipwrecks Act of 1976 with permit access controls). The diving industry throughout the country is enormous and continues to grow, with natural areas such as the Great Barrier Reef in Queensland being of international renown. The majority of located historic wreck sites (less than 10% of known national losses) are well known to local scuba divers. They generally gain first-hand site information and access details from local dive operators. All statutory agencies actively encourage diver visitation to these sites through a variety of means, including publications such as shipwreck location posters, wreck inspection reports, scholarly articles, and through lectures, displays and exhibitions, etc. A major initiative of the Australasian Institute for Maritime Archaeology (AIMA), in cooperation with the Commonwealth Historic Shipwrecks Program, has been the development of a national database of shipwreck losses. This has in quite recent times been made available to the public via the Institute's web site and linked to all state agency sites.

Individual states such as New South Wales have created other "firsts," such as the production of an A3 format *Shipwreck Atlas of NSW, Ed 3*, featuring the graphical spread of wreck sites and related technical and historic information in map form, and through unique community Wreck Survey Programs (described below). General interest publications have been encouraged by most states, including independent books covering regional shipwreck losses and particularly targeted brochures, which prove immensely popular.

But when it comes to identifying the sixty-five hundred wreck events and associated shipwreck sites "on the ground," the picture remains limited. One of the key problems has been the structure of the Commonwealth Historic Shipwrecks Program itself. There are less than twenty[1] maritime archaeology practitioners currently employed across a continent with a coastline exceeding thirty-seven thousand kilometers. Such a small pool of trained professionals therefore determines the size of a significant proportion of the available research community (Kenderdine, 1995). The quantity and quality of research data generated by this group is further constrained by their administrative responsibilities and the amount of time that can be dedicated to more holistic public education initiatives. It is not a situation that is likely to change based on the number of possible employment avenues, even taking into account the expanding range of tertiary level courses currently available in the field.

Those shipwrecks trails implemented to date have proved of interest to the general public and have attempted to fill a void regarding accessibility to the resource. Some have been highly successful in generating initial local community support, particularly by divers and school groups (see McCarthy and Garratt, 1998). However, as noted by Strachan (1995), they have been implemented in a fragmentary way as funds and time have dictated. Nationally there has been no consistency in approach, often even at a state level, nor has the development of new trails been promoted outside the borders of each state. In all states, one-off independent interpretative signs and plinths have been established for individual wreck sites and remain largely under-recognized, differing wildly in form and content, and virtually unknown as an educational or passive recreation resource (Figures 1 and 3).

---

[1] This figure takes into account full-time employment in either one of the state museum maritime archaeology programs or in a planning-based department. In addition, there are a handful of independent maritime archaeology consultants.

Some delegated agencies such as the New South Wales Heritage Office have purposely decided not to develop shipwreck trails as a part of their core business activities (personal communication, David Nutley, 1999). This acknowledges their lack of available staff resources and funds to initiate and complete successful projects, and the inability to continue the required dedicated promotion, upkeep, and expansion.

**Figure 1.** Standard shipwreck trail sign. Level of graffiti indicates problems associated with maintenance of one-off trail projects (photo by T. Smith).

Here, the agency has attempted to enlist the community, local government, and private business in the seeding of new trail and signage projects (Figure 2). To this end, it has produced a number of brochures detailing the requirements of shipwreck trail production (Heritage Office, 1995, 1998). In a similar vain, it has initiated several landmark community-based shipwreck recording programs, the 1982-1985 Wreck Survey Project and recently Wrecks Alive (1999-ongoing). These volunteer community programs encourage dive shops, clubs, and individuals to research, map, and publish independent project work and thereby encourage a community ownership and sense of responsibility for managing their local underwater (and land-based) sites. In this they have been partly successful. However, they have also been constrained by the same lack of driving force that has constrained the effectiveness of other state agency-driven shipwreck trails. Simply disseminating suitable training materials and guidelines appears insufficient to initiate and sustain successful projects.

**Figure 2.** Shipwreck trails attract significant local political and public interest (photo by T. Smith).

## 4. A NEW MODEL

If shipwreck trails have only been partially successful when organized as a key objective of state-based heritage agencies, and community-driven projects have been difficult to generate, what is the future for public access to these intriguing heritage sites? Visitors, especially non-diving visitors, currently have little choice if they seek to have an area's maritime past interpreted to them. They can visit one of a handful of regional shipwreck trails; view separate, scattered, and largely unknown plinths to one-off sites; visit a maritime museum; or gain some text-based information on the history of sites via the National Historic Shipwrecks Database. It is to a recently organized land-based signage program that a model for a more holistic educational experience might be gained.

During the convict days of New South Wales, an important arterial road was constructed by convict labor from Sydney. Known as the Great North Road, it had largely escaped conservation care, historic analysis, and community recognition since its construction between 1826 and 1834. Within a few short years, however, this two hundred and forty-kilometer heritage structure has been rejuvenated through the implementation of a dynamic program driven by community, government (national, state, and local), and educational institutions.

Known as the Convict Trail Project, it appears a useful model to be considered when formulating future regional or a national "Historic Shipwreck Trail Project." The project's strength lies in its community origins and principle ownership. Under the direction of a Project Team with annual funding obtained from major stakeholders, the project works in partnership with key government agencies charged with administering relevant heritage planning controls (e.g., NSW National Parks & Wildlife Service, The National Trust of Australia, Roads and Traffic Authority, and a range of local shire councils). Key interest groups were targeted to assist with the development and implementation of the trail and, more importantly, to continue this association long past the initial development stage. Groups include tourism and heritage organizations, academic institutions, local business, and community groups with an interest in the conservation, sound promotion, and management of the historic road.

The project has been running since its inception in 1994 and continues to grow, expand, and enlist a never-ending train of interested parties. Currently there are over twenty-five organizations involved with several hundred volunteers and professionals. There is a clear focus of the aims of the project and the extent of the trail, and it has become self-generating. It works because "by working together in a collaborative way, the various groups and organizations are able to accomplish far more than their individual actions

Figure 3. Typical one-off marker on purpose-built viewing platform overlooking the wreck of the *P.S. Manning*, NSW (photo by D. Nutley).

could have achieved" (Banks et al., 1999b). This has a benefit in sharing resources (especially staff time), spreading out financial burdens, targeting areas of immediate and crucial conservation and interpretation need, and in working closely with the regional communities through which the road passes (Banks et al., 1999b). The development of a similar team structure for the linear spread of coastal and riverine shipwreck sites (both on land and underwater in the near-shore) appears achievable. While the initial seed idea could be planted by the state agency charged with administering the National Shipwrecks Program, the acceptance of the project regionally through component "National Shipwreck Trail" committees could begin.

The Convict Trail Project has benefited from the motivation and participation of each institution, group, and individual. The sense of ownership is spread amongst a diverse range of participants. Guided by an overall Conservation Management Plan dictating site stabilization and appropriate restoration works and access, the teams also work towards an integrated Tourism and Interpretation Plan. This lays the foundation for the promotion of the heritage item in a practical way so that people can experience it at a range of levels and locations, and acquire an understanding of the role, in this case, of convict building programs.

Education initiatives have included community working bees, the implementation of on-site signage, brochures, maps, and trail guides, newsletters, annual reports, traveling exhibition materials, CD-ROMs, web sites, a database of information related to the item and the project, guided walks, extensive media coverage of achievements and talks, seminars, and workshops. Key successes have been the grass-roots community involvement in all aspects of the project and the learning experience generated for school children and the wider public, particularly by historic reenactment days.

**Figure 4.** A standard metal-photo interpretive sign used in Australia (photo by J. Smith).

Community-oriented historic research projects, guided by professional agencies such as the "Adopt a Convict" program, have been highly successful and generated further research and an interest focus (an "Adopt a Wreck" concept could be considered). The project has been successfully funded by limited government grants (federal, state, and local) and through initiatives such as the establishment of local heritage funds and donation schemes such as "The Friends of the Convict Trail."

The New South Wales Heritage Office is currently examining elements of this model in the development of promotional strategies in New South Wales. The Convict Trail concept is a model that could conceivably be applied widely to Australia's unique historic shipwreck resource and be developed throughout all coastal and riverine communities through a staged implementation approach.

Figure 5. A marker on the significant "Great Ocean Road" shipwreck trail in Victoria, Australia (photo by J. Smith).

## 5. CONCLUSION

Apart from attempting to establish community-driven comparable signage projects in tandem across the state, the Heritage Office is developing a "Maritime Heritage Online" web site in which to showcase the results. The site will also provide an electronic version of the popular *Shipwreck Atlas of New South Wales*, shipwreck research facilities, and information on related maritime heritage sites and places and how to access them.

Maritime Heritage Online will promote community leadership in preserving local built heritage, develop consistency of approach throughout regional areas, facilitate a commitment to maintain trails, and provide a focus for ongoing promotion and funding. Initiatives such as the Heritage Office's community Wreck Survey Projects and AIMA's Maritime Archaeology (NAS) Training Courses will be encouraged in an attempt to generate further grass roots interest in shipwreck management. Potential for a national wreck trails web site is also being discussed (personal communication, Bill Jeffery, 2001).

Historically, heritage trails and signage programs have concluded with the construction of the last plinth and official public launch. They are often then passed over by subsequent trail planning or agency priorities. Maintenance schedules become harder to meet unless adopted by another party, and the promotion of the trail and dissemination of accompanying illustrative material less of a priority. As noted, ongoing promotion of the resource is often unachievable due to the nature of the agencies coordinating the project.

By comparison, the Convict Trail Project has transformed what could have been a static mute display established to recollect past events. It is a working, living, thriving example of local communities interacting with their heritage sites, nurturing this new, special link with the past. It is now ready for adaptation.

# REFERENCES

Banks, L., 1999a, *Convict Trail Project: Draft Business Plan 2000-2003*, Sydney.
Banks, L., 1999b, Road Works in Progress, *Convict Trail Project Update* (newsletter), Number 7.
Budde, P., 1997, *Convict Trail Great North Road: Annual Report 1997*, Erina.
Heritage Office, 1999, *Wrecks Alive: Community Shipwreck Survey Kit*, Sydney.
Heritage Office, 1998, *Shipwreck Trails: Guidelines*, Sydney.
Heritage Office, 1996, *Shipwreck Atlas of New South Wales*, ed. 3, Sydney.
Heritage Office, 1995, *Underwater Heritage: Local Government Guidelines*, Sydney.
Heritage Office, 1995, *NSW Heritage: Guidelines for Heritage Trails*, Sydney.
Heritage Victoria, 1994, *The Discovery Coast historic shipwreck trail guide* (brochure), Melbourne.
Jeffery, B., 1990, Realising the cultural tourism potential of South Australian shipwrecks, in: *Historic Environment* 7(3):72-76.
Kenderdine, S., 1995, *Historic Shipwrecks National Research Plan*, Department of Communications and the Arts, Canberra.
McCarthy, M., 1983, Wrecks and recreation, in: *Proceedings of the Second Southern Hemisphere Conference on Maritime Archaeology*, South Australian Department of Environment and Planning, Adelaide, pp. 381-390.
McCarthy, M., and Garratt, D., 1998, The WA Maritime Museum's wreck access and outreach program, in: *Bulletin of the Australian Institute for Maritime Archaeology* 22:127-132.
Nutley, D., 1998, Ten years of shipwreck access and management practices in New South Wales, in: *Bulletin of the Australian Institute for Maritime Archaeology* 22:115-118.
Penrose, J., 1983, Education in maritime archaeology: an Australian perspective, in: *Proceedings of the Second Southern Hemisphere Conference on Maritime Archaeology*, South Australian Department of Environment and Planning, Adelaide, pp. 65-77.
Prince, B., 1997, The evaluation of the Rottnest Island trail experiment, in: *Bulletin of the Australian Institute for Maritime Archaeology* 11(1):5-6.
Punchard, E., 1992, Wreck trail identity plinths, a proposed new design for the Hamlin Bay Wreck Trail requiring minimal resource, unpublished paper, Western Australian Maritime Museum.
Robertson, E., 1990, History, heritage and interpretation: historic Quarantine Station, Manly, Sydney, in: *Locality, Bulletin of the Community History Program* 4(4):7-9.
Samuel, B., 1999, Interpreting heritage, in: *Heritage South Australia* 14:11-ff.
Strachan, S., 1995, Interpreting maritime heritage: Australian historic shipwreck trails, in: *Historic Environment* 11(4):26-35.
Wilde-Ramsing, M., 1994, Hidden beneath the waves: an underwater archaeology educational kit, Underwater Archaeology Unit, North Carolina Division of Archives and History, Kure Beach, North Carolina.

CHAPTER 11

# MARITIME HERITAGE TRAILS IN AUSTRALIA: AN OVERVIEW AND CRITIQUE OF THE INTERPRETIVE PROGRAMS

Cassandra Philippou and Mark Staniforth[*]

## 1. INTRODUCTION

As special-interest tourism, in particular cultural tourism, has become more popular the promotion and presentation of archaeological sites for the public has become increasingly common. For many decades, tourists have been able to participate in archaeological site tours and heritage trails in places like the Middle East and Europe. This phenomenon is seen increasingly in other parts of the world (see, for example, Cleere, 1984, 1989; Binks et al., 1988; Hall and McArthur, 1993; Potter, 1994; McManamon and Hatton, 2000). Initially, the presentation of archaeological artifacts and archaeological sites took the form of museum exhibits, site tours, and site open-days. In the last twenty years, however, heritage trails have become an important method of presenting a wide variety of heritage sites, enabling the public to access and enjoy these sites (Uzzell, 1989; Hosty, 1987; Tabata et.al., 1993).

Maritime archaeologists in some states of Australia have been extremely active in creating maritime heritage trails, primarily shipwreck trails, during the past twenty years. The first maritime heritage trail in Australia was the Rottnest Island Underwater Shipwreck Trail. It was developed in 1981 by Michael McCarthy from the Western Australian Maritime Museum in conjunction with the Rottnest Island Board. The trail includes underwater

---

[*] Cassandra Philippou and Mark Staniforth, Department of Archaeology, Flinders University, GPO Box 2100, Adelaide, 5001, South Australia, Australia.

135

plinths, land-based markers, and a booklet, making it accessible to diverse audiences (McCarthy and Garrett, 1998; Strachan, 1995).

State government agencies and museums in Western Australia (WA), South Australia (SA), and Victoria have been the most active in creating maritime heritage and, in particular, shipwreck trails. Western Australia has some twenty regional, thematic, and local maritime heritage trails throughout the state; South Australia has eight trails, both regional and thematic; and Victoria has at least eight small (or local) trails, some of which are now linked through two larger, regional trails. Other states and territories in Australia have established few, or no, publicly accessible maritime heritage trails.

New South Wales (NSW) has a somewhat different approach to the implementation of maritime heritage trails, which has seen local councils, historical societies, and museums being the key players in establishing maritime heritage trails in discrete regions. To date, five shipwreck trails have been produced in this way in NSW, with many interpretation signs produced for individual shipwrecks. The Northern Territory is in the process of producing its first maritime heritage trail, based in Arnhem Land (Steinburg, 2000). Queensland and Tasmania have very few maritime heritage trails, however James Cook University and local businesses on Magnetic Island have shown interest in establishing such education and tourism ventures (personal communication, Peter M. Veth, 2001). Tasmania has very good historical publications available on local wrecks (Broxham and Nash, 1998, 2000), however this information and research has yet to be effectively capitalized upon in the form of maritime heritage trails. To date the only maritime heritage trails in Tasmania are associated with shore-based whaling station sites in Adventure Bay on Bruny Island and an uncompleted shipwreck trail on King Island (Nash, 2001).

Various publications on shipwrecks and maritime heritage have been produced, particularly in Western Australia, Victoria, and Tasmania. South Australia, for example, has numerous publications available that were written by avocational authors (e.g. Christopher, 1990; Parsons, 1981; Perkins, 1988). While such publications can provide the public with valuable information, their audience is often restricted by cost and difficulty of access.

In 1983, Mike McCarthy wrote that "the archaeologist must explore ways and means of preserving and presenting wrecksites to the public...[and] must be prepared to 'show it all' to all walks of life" (McCarthy, 1983:381). The authors argue that the pursuit of this aim by maritime archaeologists has come to a grinding halt in Australia. Maritime archaeologists and underwater cultural heritage managers have stopped "exploring" the various options that are available. They have become complacent, and somewhat possessive, in their presentation of maritime archaeology in the form of maritime heritage trails. This chapter critically reviews the publications used to promote Australia's maritime heritage trails systems, and provides some comments for the development of maritime heritage trails in the future.

## 2. MARKETING OF MARITIME HERITAGE TRAILS: PROMOTIONAL MATERIAL AS THE PUBLIC FACE OF MANAGEMENT AGENCIES

The forms of promotional material produced for maritime heritage trails and wreck access throughout Australia are extremely varied and, in many respects, inconsistent. While it is not necessary for maritime heritage trails to have completely common design or construction elements, some basic consistency could benefit management programs nationally. Consistency and design elements, such as branding and linking trails into other regional tourism initiatives, have proved beneficial for the Victorian program (Strachan, 1995).

In 1995, the Commonwealth government commissioned a major review--the *National Historic Shipwrecks Research Program*--that called for a national approach to research of maritime archaeological sites and a "commitment to public education which will help to increase awareness and appreciation of historic shipwrecks in Australian waters" (Edmonds et al., 1995:xi). Subsequently, a re-definition of the educational direction of the various state programs has been suggested to promote the nation-wide importance of Australia's maritime heritage through the implementation of a *National Shipwrecks Interpretation Plan* (Smith, 2002). These suggestions have never been taken up, and this review of the existing heritage trails systems in Australia illustrates the disparities between the interpretation and promotion of maritime heritage through the existing maritime heritage trails in each state.

Since the implementation of the first maritime heritage trail at Rottnest Island, little progress has been made in the form of innovative interpretation that provides a clear national direction in the format and promotion of the trails systems. Those states that have developed some form of maritime heritage trail have frequently done so in a way that differs from the other states, such as South Australia's waterproof booklets that allow divers to take trail information onto submerged wrecksites, or Victoria's *Underwater Shipwreck Discovery Trail Kit*. Strachan (1995) provided a history of each of the trails created until 1995, and a breakdown of their major components and availability. While innovation has been occurring, rarely is one idea, however impressive it may be, transferred for use in the other states. The exception is the development of underwater concrete plinths by the Western Australia Maritime Museum that has been taken up in other states. The following section offers a state-by-state critique of the maritime heritage trails in Australia for the four states that have major maritime heritage trails: Victoria, NSW, SA, and WA. Tasmania, Queensland, and the Northern Territory are not discussed as they currently have few, or no, publicly accessible maritime heritage trails.

## 2.1. Western Australia

Western Australia's maritime archaeology program is operated through the WA Maritime Museum. More than twenty shipwreck trails cover more than fifteen hundred kilometers of coastline, from Albany in the south to Exmouth in the north, with some gaps in between. Information in the pamphlets covers roughly two hundred shipwrecks and associated relics on the Western Australian coast. The majority were produced over a five-year period, from 1991 to 1996, by work experience students from local high schools. The resulting pamphlets vary widely in the quality of information.

The graphic design is reasonably standardized through the series, with printing in dark blue or green ink on matt-finish paper of various colors. The same graphic designers have been used throughout. Most are badged with the logos of the Museum and collaborating schools or councils; the logos are noticeably absent on one of the pamphlets.

Inconsistencies are most conspicuous when reading the pamphlets as a series. Some pamphlets, such as the Albany Maritime Heritage Trail series, are comprehensive and well produced, providing good maps and overall history of the region, and incorporating land-based maritime heritage with the information on shipwrecks. Others provide good histories of the region but varying degrees of information on each wreck. Total written content ranges from one thousand words to over two thousand words; font sizes vary from as small as eight points up to eleven points; and pamphlet sizes also vary from three-fold A4 paper up to a larger, non-standard five-fold layout. Some maps lack north arrows and locality maps, thus failing to place the region in the wider context of the state.

Only about half make any reference to maritime archaeology at all. In addition, the historical significance of the wrecks to the region, state, or nation is not always clear. Details on the accessibility of the wrecks for divers and snorkelers are given in several pamphlets, but not in others. Some pamphlets provide GPS positions (strangely, in one case a GPS position is given for a wreck that is noted as "not recommended for diving!"), while others simply give a vague location. Approximately half provide links to other forms of interpretation such as other pamphlets or museum exhibits. None of the maps show the location of land-based interpretation, and only some mention whether underwater interpretation is available or not.

Nevertheless the WA wreck access program is arguably the most comprehensive in Australia in terms of the volume of pamphlets, the total distance of coastline, and number of wrecks that are covered. However, the funding provided for the promotional material seems minimal. The pamphlets have clearly been produced on a small budget, indicated by the lack of color, less expensive matte-finish paper, and the utilization of volunteer staff to produce them. The promotional material for the shipwreck and maritime heritage trails are the most widely accessible form of maritime heritage interpretation in Western Australia and they should reflect the museum's expertise in public education. While many of them have been produced, which is an achievement in itself, the inconsistencies and minimal finances invested is a reflection of the secondary importance of the public education role the museum has given the wreck access program.

Conversely, it is important to note that WA has some excellent larger publications and books available on the wrecks off the coast (Henderson, 1980; Henderson and Henderson, 1988; Cairns and Henderson, 1995; Kenderdine, 1995). Also, to date it is the only state that addresses the issue of access to wrecks for people with disabilities, producing a pamphlet in its series that highlights the trails, interpretation signs, wrecks, and exhibitions that are accessible for the physically challenged.

## 2.2. South Australia

The South Australian Maritime Heritage Program is administered by Heritage South Australia, the state government's non-Indigenous focused cultural heritage management agency. Since the program's inception in the early 1980s seven maritime heritage trails (mainly shipwrecks) have been established, covering approximately nine hundred kilometers of coastline from Port MacDonnell near the Victorian boarder to Wardang Island off the York Peninsula and including Kangaroo Island. An eighth trail at Garden Island near Port Adelaide recently was completed. Almost two hundred shipwrecks, some of which remain unlocated, are mentioned in this interpretation material.

The South Australian maritime heritage trail promotional material varies considerably in style and design. The first trail was established in the late 1980s and the promotional material was in the form of an A3 fold-out brochure printed in pink shades on gloss paper. This design was abandoned and the subsequent pamphlet became full-color A4 three-fold with pictures and maps. The next, and arguably most effective, design was used for two trails on the York Peninsula; this took the form of waterproof booklets containing historical information on the region and shipwrecks, and scale plans of accessible wreck sites (Figure 1). They also have maps indicating the location of land-based signs. Although costly to produce, these booklets are useful underwater tools and divers are likely to retain them as souvenirs.

In 2000 a booklet was produced for the newly established Southern Ocean Shipwreck Trail (Figure 1). This consists of forty-five pages of comprehensive historical information on the southeast region of the state. It provides information on the coastal townships and establishes the historical significance of many of the wrecks. Information is presented on the entire maritime heritage of the region, including jetties and lighthouses, with details on the more interesting and intriguing tales of maritime disasters on the coast. The booklet also highlights some interesting facts about the region and carefully avoids the mundane, less significant, or less historically verifiable maritime

**Figure 1.** A selection of maritime heritage trails booklets from South Australia (photo by C. Philippou and M. Schlitz).

incidents. It was produced as a travelling guide, to be read on the long stretches between townships, and to this end it can be useful, however there are some disadvantages. This form of promotional material automatically excludes members of the public who do not wish to undertake a great deal of reading or who cannot afford to invest the money to purchase it. Conversely, it does make a delightful souvenir. The absence of a colorful and eye-catching front cover also excludes members of the public who do not have an interest in history.

The SA trails program achieves some things better than its WA counterpart. Overall, the professional quality of the interpretation is apparent. Each pamphlet makes reference to other interpretation that is available, such as land-based signs, underwater plinths, and other trails that have been produced through the program. All are badged with Heritage SA's logo and, where available, references to further reading are supplied.

The lack of consistent design of the interpretive material that has been produced in South Australia can be considered detrimental to the maritime heritage program. It appears that the agency had difficulty deciding who their target market was: divers, non-divers, heritage tourists, or general tourists. However, given the lengthy period of time over which these pamphlets and booklets have been produced, this discrepancy can be deemed reasonable. The opportunity now arises for a more consistent style of pamphlet to be produced for trails in the future.

## 2.3. Victoria

The Victorian Historic Shipwrecks Program is operated by the Maritime Heritage Unit of Heritage Victoria. Victoria's eight maritime heritage trails cover over three hundred kilometers of coastline, and two major regional trails linking some of the smaller trails have been completed in the last decade; two pamphlets have even had second, improved editions published. The trails extend from Beware Reef in the east to the South Australian border in the west.

All of the pamphlets have been printed in color (some full color, some two or three color) on gloss-finish paper. Some are on three-fold A4 paper, while others are A3 size with three or four folds and can be opened to reveal a color poster. Each pamphlet contains various types of information, usually with a map, and color underwater and artifact photographs. One pamphlet also contains plans of the wreck sites and visual transits to allow for re-location. All material is badged with Heritage Victoria's logo and each one highlights the legal protection of historic shipwrecks and outlines the role of Heritage Victoria.

Over the last five years Heritage Victoria has produced several small, glossy publications on shipwrecks off their coast, including one on the shipwrecks at Port Phillip Heads (Anderson, 1997) and another on the history of the *City of Launceston* excavations (Strachan, 2000). They have also produced the *Underwater Shipwreck Discovery Trail Kit*, published in 1992, which is a collection of forty-two pamphlets on shipwrecks around the coast, each presented in a waterproof sleeve. There are two pamphlets per shipwreck: one describes the history and construction details of the vessel and, where possible, links the shipwreck into a trail; the second provides information on diving conditions, transits (where available), a description, and plan of the site. The pamphlets are all A4 size with blue printing on pale green, matt-finish paper. They are similar in design to the Western Australian series, but are far more cohesive and well written.

The Victorian program appears to have fewer faults and inconsistencies than the other states. Indeed, the larger regional trails are a drawcard for the towns, encouraging local communities and businesses to identify with and support the trails in their region. The Shipwreck and Discovery Coast Trails also have in their favor the popularity of the picturesque Great Ocean Road, which entices travelers away from the more direct route between Adelaide and Melbourne.

Given that the Victorian trails end at the South Australian border and the South Australian trails begin less than thirty kilometers to the west, an opportunity exists for the extension of these trails into South Australia, or certainly the capacity to cross-reference the individual publications. If the trails were aligned in some manner, such as badging or design, the result would be a six hundred kilometer continuous maritime heritage trail beginning at Moonlight Head, Victoria, and ending at the Coorong, South Australia. The stretches on either side could also be developed, and the trail between Melbourne and Adelaide promoted as Australia's longest continuous maritime heritage trail.

### 2.4. New South Wales

The New South Wales shipwrecks program's approach to maritime heritage trails is very different than the other states. Smith (2002:4), quoting David Nutley, states that the "NSW Heritage Office have purposely decided not to develop trails as a part of their core business activities." Instead, they have published guidelines for community groups and local government to develop trails in their regions, and they also provide pamphlets on various aspects of shipwreck heritage in NSW. They have a shipwrecks kit available for divers and other interested community members who want to become involved in surveying wrecks.

There are three trails in Newcastle developed by a consortium of local community groups as part of a Shipwreck Walk that promotes the maritime heritage of the city. The three walks are presented on a single pamphlet and, while it is colorful, it does not contain any photographs or a scale map. Instead, the pamphlet folds out to reveal a cartoon-style drawing of Newcastle, failing to give a clear indication of the distances between each trail. It also does not specify where interpretation signs for the trails are located.

Another five trails, spread intermittently over more than six hundred kilometers, have been established by local museums, councils, historical societies, and national parks (Figure 2). One of these trails is a series of bronze plaques displayed at a seaside shopping mall. Others consist of land-based signs, underwater plaques, or both. No pamphlets have been produced to promote these trails.

The Heritage Office of NSW also publishes guidelines for producing heritage walks and plaques. A high level of design freedom is permitted, perhaps to encourage community groups to become involved with the program and to retain a level of ownership over the trails. This can result in a variety of styles of trails and publications and, as has been stated, some trails do not have any publicity at all.

The NSW Heritage Office also publishes the NSW Historic Shipwrecks Series which contains information on the Wreck Survey Project and twelve A4 size pamphlets on various shipwrecks off the NSW coast. These pamphlets

**Figure 2.** Information on local shipwrecks is incorporated into Randwick City Council's coastal walk sign at Maroubra Beach, New South Wales (photo by C. Philippou).

contain all the appropriate information that should be presented on a shipwreck interpretation pamphlet: a description and history of the shipwreck, a sketch of the type of vessel, a location map, and a description and plan of the wrecksite. It also contains a statement reminding divers that they should not interfere with or cause any damage to a wrecksite. These pamphlets would be a good example for groups creating heritage trails. They also already have a recognizable badge that could be reproduced in all shipwreck public interpretation in NSW.

## 3. DISCUSSION: DIVERSE METHODS OF INTERPRETATION

Some of the variety of maritime heritage trails promotional material available in Australia has been outlined above. It is clear that there are several approaches to the creation of accessible public education information by the various maritime heritage management agencies. This diversity may be viewed an expression of the differing primary functions of the museums, heritage management agencies, and national parks services that house the units responsible for the historic shipwrecks programs. The main distinctions may arise from the fact that museums have research and exhibit based functions, heritage management agencies are concerned primarily with site management and enforcement, and national parks services focus on conservation and preservation.

Three out of the four states that have created maritime heritage trails as part of their "public education" program are cultural heritage management agencies. Public interpretation and education is often perceived as vital to the conservation and management of sites by the public sector (see Hall and McArthur, 1993; Tabata et al., 1993; Pearson and Sullivan, 1995). The use of quality interpretation to assist in the conservation and preservation of sites can be extremely beneficial to both the short- and long-term aims of management agencies.

None of the agencies at present have moved beyond the printed word. All interpretation is presented in the format of pamphlets, signs, booklets, books, and kits. Although a little more expensive, at least initially, the move has not been made into multi-media except for some material available through the Internet. The opportunity to use short-wave radio or cassettes for local or regional shipwreck interpretation has not been exploited. Nor have CD-ROMs for virtual tours of shipwrecks been used. Some of these innovations have been used in other areas for nearly a decade (De Young, 1992) and await exploration by maritime archaeologists in Australia.

Nutley, in 1987, expressed his view of the requirements of "interpretation" of maritime heritage sites. He stated that interpretation should be "provocative and challenging," it should attempt to "break down negative attitudes and indifference towards underwater cultural heritage" and "foster national pride and identity" (1987:30). He also declares that interpretation should illustrate the significance of shipwrecks and other maritime heritage to modern life through their "aesthetic appeal, and [also as] a means of understanding human behaviour and our own society" (Nutley 1987:30).

While there are many varieties of interpretation, the production of free or inexpensive flyers, pamphlets, and booklets are arguably the most accessible. Certainly, interpretation does take other forms, such as underwater plinths, on-site signage, and larger books and publications. However, pamphlets and similar publications should be aiming to achieve all the objectives that Nutley outlines. Professional interpreters, such as Currie and Var (1992:70), hold a similar view:

> Interpretation should not just mean a run-down of the history of the site. Interpretation should also encompass the importance of the site's preservation, and importance of it in the history of the region, in the past, and for the future.

Again, in 1996, this point is highlighted by Nutley who asserts that "on-site interpretive facilities are...developed to encourage divers not only to visit a site, but to appreciate and actively protect its heritage values" (1996:102-103). They certainly should aim to do this and interpretative facilities can encourage divers to visit sites, and often to appreciate them, but does interpretation encourage divers to protect the heritage values? The pamphlets for the maritime heritage trails that have been examined above often say little about the "real" heritage values of the site or suite of sites.

While these views have been aired in the past (Nutley, 1987, 1996; Strachan, 1995; Smith 2002), this critique of the trails systems in Australia has illustrated that many of the challenges in interpretation are yet to be met. Maritime heritage trails interpretation is rarely "provocative and challenging," and so often is simply a "rundown of the history of the site[s]"--the sites' significance is rarely expressed in a manner that makes it evident to the majority of the public.

The inconsistencies in the approaches, from no trails or publications, to trails with large, costly publications, are also problematic. This illustrates one of the major flaws in the trails systems: the inability to identify the target audience. It seems that the basic research for the implementation of trails programs has not been undertaken in a thorough fashion. Are the pamphlets designed to target children, adults, the general public, or special interest groups such as divers? This is possibly the explanation for the many different styles that have been attempted. However, agencies need to endeavor to cover all or as many of these groups as possible. Many of the publications automatically limit their audience by lack of color, too much text, and a tedious focus on historical detail; the audiences who miss out are often children and those who do not have a specific interest in history. In addition, the pamphlets frequently restrict their audience through lack of information, such as how to get to the region or how long it takes to complete the walk or drive. In some cases they even exclude divers by not providing site descriptions and information about accessibility.[1]

Smith highlights a second issue that the trails are rarely promoted outside of the local or regional areas (Smith, 2002:4). This was seen by Strachan as an "under-utilisation of promotional avenues and networks available through the tourism industry," inhibited by heritage managers' "lack of expertise in marketing and promotion" (1995:29). In order to promote the preservation and protection of maritime heritage sites to as many and varied audiences as possible, managers must take full advantage of the opportunities made available through widely accessible publicity. Distribution of promotional

---

[1] It is essential to note here that many trails publications also encompass individual sites where more extensive research and interpretation of the history and resource have been undertaken. Sites such as *Clan Ranald* in South Australia, *William Salthouse* in Victoria, and numerous others are all part of larger existing trails; further information is available on these sites, often in the form of small A4 pamphlets.

material should not be limited to the direct location concerned; pamphlets ought to be made available at tourist locations and information centers in the city as well as throughout the regions being promoted.

Strachan's review of the development of maritime heritage trails in Australia in 1995 noted that another major problem was the limited post-production support. She states that, "most of the energies of participants put into creating a trail goes into creating the product, not selling it...[these dissolve] after the product is completed" (1995:29). This applies not only to the maintenance of the trails but also to publication of second editions and the encouragement of wider accessibility of the trails publicity beyond the specific location (Strachan, 1995:29).

Both of these issues were made evident when undertaking the research to write this chapter: many of the pamphlets are out of print and plans for re-prints have not been made. Also, when looking for promotional pamphlets on one of the newest trails in South Australia (The Port Elliot Trail) they could not be found in any of the more obvious locations, such as the local museum and interpretive center, and the manager and volunteer staff of the center had no knowledge of the Trail at all.

This brings this chapter to one final point. In order for a heritage trail of any kind to be successful, community involvement is vital. Some of the trails around South Australia have been cooperative ventures between community groups and the management agency. Community ownership over a trail is just as important as community stewardship over the sites themselves, and these two objectives can be circular and self-affirming. The local or regional community should be consulted regarding the location of the trail and the amount of interpretation that is required, not only for the on-site signage but also for the promotional and supplementary materials. The community may also have a local museum display or exhibition that could be linked into the trail to provide a more holistic experience for the visitors.

This level of community involvement in the Shipwreck Coast trail has worked well for Victoria (Strachan, 1995), and the South Australian agency is currently in negotiations with the Edithburg community on the York Peninsula to involve them in further interpretation of the *Clan Ranald* site (Arnott, 2001).

## 4. CONCLUSION

Many maritime archaeologists in Australia have commented on the need for public interpretation of the shipwreck resource (McCarthy, 1983; Nutley, 1987; Jeffery, 1990a; Strachan, 1995; McCarthy and Garrett, 1998; Smith, 2002). Most also note that cultural tourism, in its many forms, is a major consumer of maritime heritage interpretation and that it is important to cater to the many, varied groups of tourists who are interested in cultural sites.

In order to ensure that the publicity for maritime heritage trails is effective, it is imperative that an ample investment of time and resources is made. If the general public are not educated about the importance of shipwrecks and other maritime heritage in the history and future of their region, state, or nation, it is unlikely that these "cultural resources" will survive. It is time now for maritime archaeologists in Australia to bring cohesion to the interpretation that is provided for the public and to employ techniques that will ensure that the all members of the public get the most from their interaction with Australia's maritime heritage.

# REFERENCES

Anderson, R., 1997, *Wrecks on the Reef: A Guide to the Historic Shipwrecks at Port Phillip Heads*, Heritage Council Victoria, Melbourne, Victoria.
Arnott, T., 2001, *History of the Clan Ranald*, paper presented at the Wardang Island Field School, Port Victoria, South Australia.
Binks, G., Dyke, J., and Dagnall, P., 1988, *Visitors Welcome: A Manual on the Presentation and Interpretation of Archaeological Excavations*, H.M.S.O., London.
Broxham, G., and Nash, M., 1998, *Tasmanian Shipwrecks, Volume 1: 1797-1899*, Navarine Publishing, Woden, ACT.
Broxham, G., and Nash, M., 2000, *Tasmanian Shipwrecks, Volume 2: 1900-1999*, Navarine Publishing, Woden, ACT.
Cairns, L., and Henderson, G., 1995, *Unfinished Voyages: Western Australian Shipwrecks 1881-1900*, University of Western Australia Press, Nedlands, Western Australia.
Christopher, P., 1990, *South Australian Shipwrecks 1802-1989: A Database*, Society for Underwater Historical Research, North Adelaide, South Australia.
Cleere, H. (ed.), 1984, *Approaches to the Archaeological Heritage: A Comparative Study of World Cultural Resource Management Systems*, Cambridge University Press, Cambridge.
Cleere, H. (ed.), 1989, *Archaeological Heritage Management in the Modern World*, Unwin Hyman, London.
Currie, R. R., and Var, T., 1992, Nature and historic-based tourism, in: *Joining Hands for Quality Tourism: Interpretation, Preservation and the Travel Industry*, R. S. Tabata, J. Yamashira, and G. Cherem (eds.), *Proceedings of the Heritage Interpretation International $3^{rd}$ Global Congress*, University of Hawaii Sea Grant Extension Service, Honolulu, Hawaii, pp. 73-76.
De Young, B., 1992, A promising "distance learning" technology for coastal resource interpretation, in: *Joining Hands for Quality Tourism: Interpretation, Preservation and the Travel Industry*, R. S. Tabata, J. Yamashira, and G. Cherem (eds.), *Proceedings of the Heritage Interpretation International $3^{rd}$ Global Congress*, University of Hawaii Sea Grant Extension Service, Honolulu, Hawaii, pp. 83-85.
Edmonds, L., Kenderdine, S., Nayton, G., and Staniforth, M., 1995, National Historic Shipwrecks Research Plan, Department of Communication and the Arts, Canberra, ACT.
Hall, C. M., and McArthur, S. (eds.), 1993, *Heritage Management in New Zealand and Australia*, Oxford University Press, Auckland, New Zealand.
Henderson, G., 1980, *Unfinished Voyages: Western Australian Shipwrecks 1622-1850*, University of Western Australia Press, Nedlands, Western Australia.
Henderson, G., and Henderson, K. J., 1988, *Unfinished Voyages: Western Australian Shipwrecks 1851-1880*, University of Western Australia Press, Nedlands, Western Australia.
Hosty, K., 1987, Historic shipwrecks legislation & the Australian diver: past, present & future, *The Bulletin of the Australian Institute for Maritime Archaeology* 11(1):21-25.
Jeffery, B., 1990a, A future direction of maritime archaeology in South Australia, *The Bulletin of the Australian Institute for Maritime Archaeology* 14(2):35-40.
Jeffery, B., 1990b, Realising the cultural tourism potential of South Australian shipwrecks, *Historic Environment* VII (3/4):72-76.
Kenderdine, S., 1995, *Shipwrecks 1656-1942: A Guide to Historic Shipwrecks of Perth, W.A.*, Department of Maritime Archaeology, Western Australian Maritime Museum, Fremantle, Western Australia.
McCarthy, M., 1983, Wrecks and recreation, in: *Proceedings of the Second Southern Hemisphere Conference on Maritime Archaeology*, B. Jeffery and J. Amess (eds.), Department of Planning, South Australian and the Department of Home Affairs, Adelaide, South Australia, pp. 381-390.
McCarthy, M., 1997, Australian maritime archaeology: changes, their antecedents and the path ahead, *Australian Archaeology* 47:3-38.
McCarthy, M., and Garrett, D., 1998, The Western Australian Maritime Museum's wreck access and outreach program, *The Bulletin of the Australian Institute for Maritime Archaeology* 22:127-132.

McManamon, F. P., and Hatton, A. (eds.), 2000, *CRM in Contemporary Society: Perspectives on Managing and Presenting the Past*, Routledg, London.

Nash, M., 2001, maritime heritage trails in Tazmania, email communication to C. Philippou, June 1, 2001.

Nutley, D., 1987, Maritime heritage protection: education as the long arm of the law, *The Bulletin of the Australian Institute for Maritime Archaeology* 11(1):29-33.

Nutley, D., 1996, Underwater Cultural Heritage Management, in: *Issues in Management Archaeology, Tempus*, Vol. 5, L. J. Smith and A. Clarke (eds.), University of Queensland, St Lucia, Queensland, pp. 99-105.

Parsons, R. H., 1981, *Shipwrecks in South Australia: 1836-1875*, R. H. Parsons, Magill, South Australia.

Pearson, M., and Sullivan, S., 1995, *Looking after Heritage Places: The Basics of Heritage Planning for Managers, Landowners and Administrators*, Melbourne University Press, Melbourne, Victoria.

Perkins, J., 1988, *The Shipwrecks of Port Elliot 1853-64*, Society for Underwater Historical Research, Adelaide, South Australia.

Potter, P. B., 1994, *Public Archaeology in Annapolis: A critical Approach to History in Maryland's Ancient City*, Smithsonian Institution Press, Washington, D.C.

Smith, T., 2003, Shipwreck Trails: Public Ownership of a Unique Resource? – An Australian Perspective, this volume.

Steinberg, D., 2000, The maritime culture of a struggling port: A study of early Darwin through the history of the SS *Brisbane*, unpublished paper presented at Australian Institute for Maritime Archaeology & Australasian Society for Historical Archaeology Joint Conference - *Archaeology, Heritage and Tourism Conference*, Adelaide, South Australia.

Strachan, S., 1995, Interpreting maritime heritage: Australian historic shipwreck trails, in: *Historic Environment* 11(4):26-35.

Strachan, S., 2000, *Silts in the Sight Glass: Protectors and Raiders of the SS City of Launceston 1863-1865*, Heritage Victoria, Melbourne, Victoria.

Tabata, R. S., Yamashira, J., and Cherem, G. (eds.), 1993, *Joining hands for quality tourism: interpretation, preservation and the travel industry*, Proceedings of the Heritage Interpretation International 3$^{rd}$ Global Congress, University of Hawaii Sea Grant Extension Service, Honolulu, Hawaii.

Uzzell, D., (ed.), 1989, *Heritage Interpretation, Volumes 1 & 2*, Belhaven Press, New York.

CHAPTER 12

# FLORIDA KEYS NATIONAL MARINE SANCTUARY SHIPWRECK TRAIL: A MODEL FOR MULTIPLE-USE RESOURCE MANAGEMENT

Bruce G. Terrell[*]

## 1. INTRODUCTION

With the continental United State's only tropical coral reef, the Florida Keys hold many charms for both recreational and scientific divers. Besides unique biological resources, the Keys are the site of several hundred historic ship sinkings that date as far back as the seventeenth century.

The Florida Keys formally joined the National Oceanic and Atmospheric Administration's (NOAA) National Marine Sanctuary Program in 1998. In addition to managing the diverse natural resources, NOAA also manages the submerged historical and archaeological resources in partnership with the State of Florida.

The National Marine Sanctuary Program is guided by the National Marine Sanctuary Act of 1972. The sanctuaries promote comprehensive management of special ecological, historical, recreational, and aesthetic marine resources. Sanctuaries may be designated in coastal and ocean waters and in the U.S. Great Lakes. To date there are thirteen National Marine Sanctuaries.

Since there are as many varied users of the marine environment as there are resources to protect, the Sanctuary Act seeks to balance these multiple uses with the primary goal of resource protection. The program's mission is to manage areas of special national significance through stewardship, education, and research programs that foster public understanding, support, and

---

[*] Bruce G. Terrell, National Oceanic and Atmospheric Administration, Marine Sanctuary Division, 1305 East-West Highway, 12th Floor, Silver Spring, Maryland 20910.

participation, and that promote ecologically sustainable use of the nation's natural and cultural marine resources.

To clearly define the Florida Keys National Marine Sanctuary's (FKNMS) responsibility towards archaeological resources, NOAA entered into a programmatic agreement with Florida's Department of State. Among the many points that were addressed, it was agreed that the parties would "work toward establishing a system of underwater parks and underwater shipwreck trails where public access [would] be encouraged." (Programmatic Agreement 1998:8-9) (Figure 1).

In anticipation of this requirement, NOAA's Sanctuary Program began developing the Florida Keys NMS Shipwreck Trail in 1995; the goals were

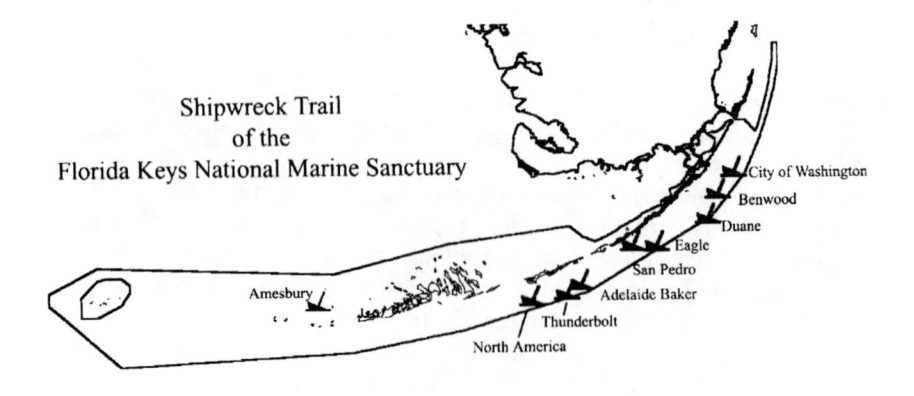

**Figure 1.** FKNMS Shipwreck Trail map.

several. The project was envisioned primarily as an educational project to inform visitors and locals, alike, about the maritime history and material culture associated with the Florida Keys.

Another goal of the Trail was to ease diver pressure on the natural environment. The Florida Keys are one of the largest sport diving destinations in the United States. In addition to many natural and man-made threats, the reefs are in danger of being "loved to death." The Shipwreck Trail was envisioned as a possible vehicle to steer some percentage of divers away from the reefs.

One other goal is to study the wrecks as artificial reefs. The microenvironments that are established soon after a ship's sinking provide useful information to aid in the restoration of reefs that are damaged in ship groundings.

The Keys have bordered major historical shipping routes for centuries. Between the sixteenth and eighteenth centuries, Spanish treasure fleets, called *flotas*, skirted the Keys as they sailed northward seeking favorable currents that would speed them to Spain. In July 1733, a *flota* consisting of five armed galleons and eighteen other merchant ships was driven against the Keys' reef by a hurricane causing the loss of all but one vessel. Several modern salvors have since gained renown or, in some cases, notoriety by salvaging most of this fleet beginning with Art McKee in 1937. Another famous alumnus of the Keys' treasure controversy was the late Mel Fisher.

In the nineteenth century ships transited the region to and from Gulf of Mexico ports including New Orleans, Louisiana, and Galveston, Texas. Numerous ships from both Europe and the U.S. that visited these ports were lost in the Keys. Bahamian and American wrecking camps were established along the largely uninhabited Keys to salvage wrecked ships. A U.S. Customs House was eventually built at the burgeoning town of Key West to monitor the wrecking industry. The high loss rate caused the U.S. to erect many navigational aids to curb the losses. The remains of several nineteenth-century light houses and channel markers may still be seen on the seabed.

Watercraft involved in U.S. coastal and Caribbean trade also passed the Keys. Small sloops and schooners from the Bahamas, Cuba, and Key West were engaged in regional coastal trade, sponge fishing, and other local fisheries. The Key West Smack is an example of a unique small craft developed by the local fishing industry in the nineteenth century. All mariners sailed with wariness of the lethal submerged reefs and shoals of the Keys' island chain and many were lost. The deceptively placid region became dangerous when hurricanes seemingly erupted without warning in the days before accurate weather prediction.

Military activities, too, claimed ships during the many European and American naval conflicts that played in the area. During the late eighteenth and early nineteenth centuries, pirates and privateers played hide-and-seek with the U.S. Navy among the mangrove-veiled islands. A locally known wreck site is the supposed remains of the American patrol schooner USS *Alligator* which sank in 1822. Several Civil War-era vessels sank in the region including the troopship *Menemon Sanford* which sank in the Carysfort Light region. Victims of World War II German U-boat predation are also to be found in the deeper waters of the Keys.

## 2. SHIPWRECK PRESERVE CONCEPTS

For some time now, submerged cultural resource management agencies have developed shipwreck preserves in attempts to make these historical resources accessible to the diving public. Preserves have proven to be excellent ways to provide educational experiences to communities on topics ranging from regional history to historic preservation and on the importance of low-impact diving in protecting underwater resources (Figure 2).

The 1987 Abandoned Shipwreck Act recommended such preserve development. The Abandoned Shipwreck Act Guidelines contained several recommendations to assist shipwreck preserve creation. Guidelines include:

- Consultation with various interest groups in early developmental stages.
- Preparation of environmental and economic impact assessments of proposed sites.
- Definition of the preserve's purpose, significance, boundaries, and special conditions and constraints.
- Development of management plans.
- Interpretation and facilitation of public access to shipwreck sites.
- Protection of shipwreck sites.

From the beginning and throughout the Florida Keys Shipwreck Trail process, NOAA consulted other wreck preserve projects as models. Early on, NOAA considered work accomplished by Charles Beeker and Indiana University's Underwater Science Education and Research program's field schools to document sites in the Keys for Florida's Bureau of Archaeological Research. Several of those sites were included in the Shipwreck Trail. Several pre-existing state preserve systems also were consulted, including preserves developed by Florida's Bureau of Archaeological Research, at Vermont's Lake Champlain, at New York's Lake George, and those developed by Michigan's Bottomland Preserve Program.

AN ADVENTURE
TO DIVE FOR...
**Figure 2.** Shipwreck Trail brochure cover.

Prior to identifying potential sites, NOAA developed lists of criteria, potential partners, and critical issues that followed the Abandoned Shipwreck Act Guidelines. Briefly, here are some of the issues that were considered.

## 2.1. Partners

The sanctuary designation process had made it clear that there was some community resistance to the designation of the Florida Keys National Marine Sanctuary. NOAA officials knew going into the Trail program that the project would be doomed unless there was local diver and merchant support. Dive shops, charter operators, and even the old-time salvors were consulted for their suggestions. The local Keys Association of Dive Operators (KADO) became one of NOAA's main partners in selecting sites and in helping to reach the dive community.

NOAA's primary partner was the State of Florida's Division of Historical Resources, which helped to design the program and to secure funds and grant moneys including National Historic Preservation Grants and State Education Grants. Other partners that helped NOAA to realize the project were the Nature Conservancy, Pigeon Key Foundation, and the Florida Department of Environmental Protection.

## 2.2. Products

The products that we wanted to produce included:

- Waterproof diver guides for each wreck site.
- An overall interpretive brochure.
- Anchoring and site identification buoys (Figure 3).
- Plans for the later development of a land-side interpretive exhibit for diving and non-diving visitors.
- A community outreach program.

**Figure 3.** Shipwreck Trail identification buoy.

## 2.3. Themes

The Shipwreck Trail team identified several overall themes that were important to impart to visitors. Themes included:
[double space?]

- Historic ship architecture - site guides would help to identify structural features within wreck remains.
- Historic events - incidents associated with Keys maritime history.
- Site aesthetics - provide aesthetic experiences and also good photographic backgrounds for photographers.
- Historic preservation message - educate divers about the value of historic preservation to the public.
- Self-policing community protection - since Sanctuary enforcement is limited in its capabilities, divers are encouraged to help protect the sites from the irresponsible few by reporting incidents of vandalism.
- A sensitive diving message - educate divers about the importance of controlling buoyancy, fin activity, etc.
- Interpretation – educate divers about natural resources that have colonized the wrecks.

## 2.4. Site Selection

The process of selecting wrecks for the Trail was of paramount importance. NOAA wanted to select sites that had educational and aesthetic value. However, the sites needed to be relatively non-sensitive and capable of handling increased visitor traffic.

## 2.5. Site Protection

A critical element in shipwreck preserves is the provision of spar buoys for site identification and mooring buoys for dive boats. Anchoring is always a threat to the integrity of an underwater resource. NOAA also decided to preserve site aesthetics by not putting plaques or markers at the wreck site.

## 3. SITE IDENTIFICATION

Twelve prospective sites were identified for possible inclusion on the Trail. Contracts were let for three companies to document sites in the three regions of the Sanctuary, the Key Largo region, the Middle Keys around Marathon, and the Lower Keys near Key West. The resulting data were used to aid in site selection as well as to prepare interpretive materials. From the initial twelve, nine sites made the final selection for inclusion; the following is a brief discussion of their histories.

*City of Washington* was a steel-hulled ship built by John Roach & Sons at Chester, Pennsylvania, in 1877. The ship operated in the Caribbean and Gulf of Mexico as a passenger and cargo steamer. The *City of Washington* was at anchor in Havana, Cuba, when the USS *Maine* blew up in February of 1898, and was the first vessel on the scene to rescue survivors. During the ensuing Spanish-American War, the *Washington* was used as a troop transport between Florida and Cuba. While operating in the New York to Cuba trade in 1917 she ran aground on The Elbow Reef in the upper Florida Keys while under tow. Today, about 325 feet of the lower hull is in place. Engine mounts, various fittings, and the vessel's iron knees may be seen both in place and in scattered proximity to the wreck. In addition to its historical significance, the site provides a good representation of period steel-hulled construction techniques. This wreck is also an excellent site to see various corals and fish species.

Located one mile northeast of French Reef in the upper Keys are the remains of the steel freighter *Benwood*, built in 1910. The *Benwood* sank in a night-time collision during wartime blackout conditions in 1942. The site was subject to many salvage attempts and was a military bombing target in the 1950s and, consequently, has much material scattered about the site. Its easily accessed location in twenty-five feet of water make *Benwood* one of the most popular dive sites in the Florida Keys.

The *Duane*, a retired Coast Guard Cutter built in 1937, was sunk as an artificial reef in 1987 by the Keys Association of Dive Operators. *Duane* was a 327-feet-long Treasury Class cutter and saw service during World War II as an anti-submarine vessel. The ship had the distinction of being the only Coast Guard ship to serve as a flagship during the war, for an Amphibious Task Group in Operation Dragoon during the invasion of southern France in August 1944. The *Duane* continued to serve the Coast Guard until her retirement in 1985, at that time the oldest active U.S. military vessel in service. She now lies upright on a sand bottom at a depth of one hundred twenty feet (Figure 4).

Built in Holland in 1962, the *Eagle Tire Company*, now *Eagle*, does not qualify as a historic shipwreck but has been included for its aesthetic and recreational value. The *Eagle* accidentally sank at its present location as it was being prepared for sinking as an artificial reef in 1985.

Not all of the Shipwreck Trail is composed of twentieth-century steel-hulled ships. The site of the remains of the eighteenth-century Spanish ship *San Pedro* is a State of Florida Underwater Archaeological Preserve designated in 1989. Site elements include a ballast pile, replica cannons, an anchor moved from a different contemporary wreck, and a bronze interpretive

# Duane

Diver Level: Advanced Openwater
Maximum Depth: 125 feet
Location: 24-59.388N, 80-22.888W

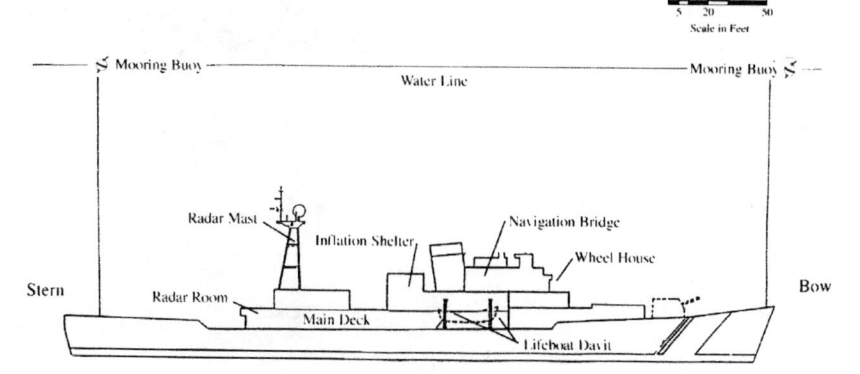

**Figure 4.** *Duane* plan.

plaque. The *San Pedro* was part of the previously noted treasure fleet disaster from 1733. Designated for its historical value, the *San Pedro* serves to represent the appearance of the numerous ballast piles of wooden shipwrecks that lie in the Keys. Ballast piles often preserve the few wooden hull remains that have escaped salvors' ravages.

The fragmentary iron remains of what is thought to be the three-masted wooden bark *Adelaide Baker* are found on the Coffin's Patch Reef off Marathon in the middle Keys. She was built as the *F. Carver* in Bangor, Maine, in 1863 and sank under British ownership as the *Baker* in 1889. The *Baker* is an example of late nineteenth-century transitional wooden ships that incorporated iron frames and masts and wire rigging. The site is strewn with several iron masts, two water tanks, deadeyes, numerous hanging knees, knee riders, and many other fittings. The two areas of artifact concentration indicate the possible collection activities of contemporary and modern salvors (Figure 5).

**Figure 5.** *Adelaide Baker* site map.

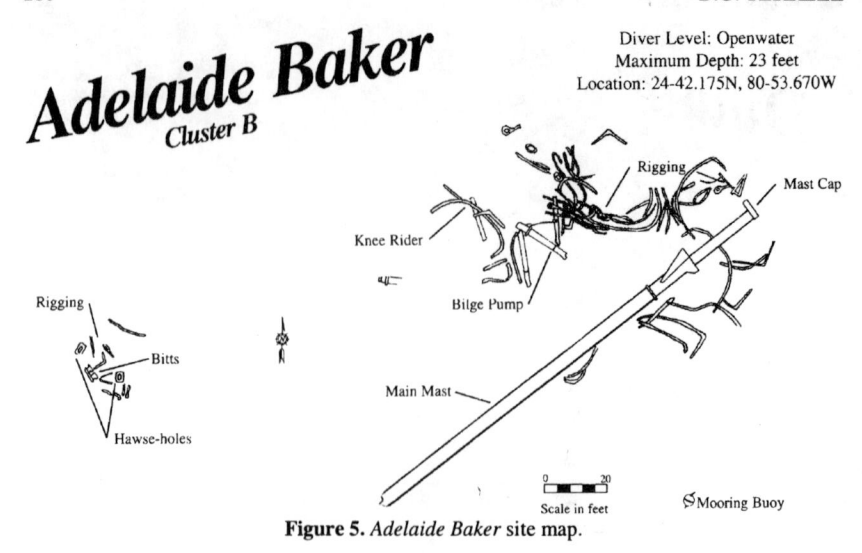

    This site, while not aesthetically pretty, is useful for interpreting the construction of this period of ship building (Figure 6). The knee riders are particularly useful for illustrating the cross-section profile of the ship's hull. The site is also illustrative of the context-destroying activities of unregulated treasure hunting in the past.

    The *Thunderbolt* was originally the 189-feet-long mine layer *Randolph* built in Point Pleasant, West Virginia, in 1942 for the U.S. Army Coast Artillery Corps. The ship was purchased by the Florida Power and Light Company and was used as a research vessel to test electrical energy in lightning strikes, hence the name *Thunderbolt*. Sunk as an artificial reef, like several of the Shipwreck Trail vessels to the north, *Thunderbolt* serves to illustrate twentieth-century steel ship construction. The site also contains much interesting biota and attracts many fish species.

    Off Marathon's Delta Shoals lie the remains of the lower floor and ballast of what is believed to be the mid-nineteenth-century down-easter

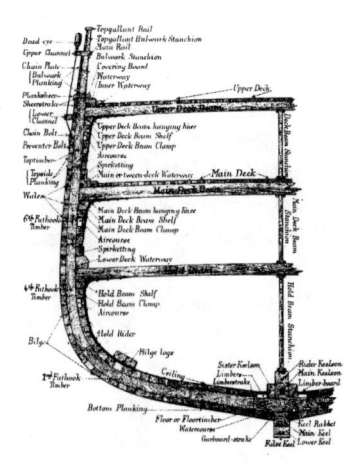

**Figure 6.** Composite hull construction (Paasch, 1997).

*North America.* The site contains most of the lower hull between the cant frames and the stern, although neither of those two features are present. The site is useful for interpreting the construction features of wooden vessels from the early nineteenth century.

A ship, known locally as Alexander's Wreck, was found by the Shipwreck Trail team to be the remains of the U.S. Naval Destroyer Escort *Amesbury*. Built in 1943, *Amesbury* escorted North Atlantic convoys and earned a battle star for her participation in the Normandy Invasion. She was later converted into a high-speed transport and served in the Pacific theater and later in the Korean conflict. After decommissioning and use as a sunken target, *Amesbury* was raised and sold to a Key West salvage company for scrap. Now in two sections, the forward half is the most recognizable part of the vessel. The site contains many interesting features including a five-inch gun mount and several twin forty-millimeter Bofors antiaircraft gun mounts.

## 4. FUTURE OF THE SHIPWRECK TRAIL

The Florida Keys National Marine Sanctuary is hindered by the lack of a staff Marine Archaeologist. To date, the Sanctuary has relied upon the benevolence of several talented volunteers but needs a staff professional who can design a monitoring program that can calculate diver use and assess diver impact and stress on the sites. The initial sites were chosen primarily because they were deemed rugged enough to handle diver traffic. However, before new sites are designated that may be more illustrative but are also more fragile, the program needs to construct and implement a sound monitoring and management plan.

The program also needs to follow the designation of the Sanctuary with a solid community education program. A land-side exhibit is tentatively planned and the Sanctuary needs knowledgeable speakers to reach out to the community to educate the public about the Trail and to encourage their support. Other types of outreach should include popular publications, a web site, and solid management-based reporting.

The Florida Keys Shipwreck Trail has made a good start with the designation of the wreck sites. It now needs to follow through with an on-going program that can satisfy both visitor and local community needs.

## REFERENCES

Paasch, 1997 (reprint of 1885 edition), *Paasch's Illustrated Marine Dictionary*, Lyon and Burford Publishers, New York.

Programmatic Agreement among the National Oceanic and Atmospheric Administration, the Advisory Council on Historic Preservation, and the State of Florida for Historical Resource Management in the Florida Keys National Marine Sanctuary, 1998, III.D.3.

CHAPTER 13

# MARITIME HERITAGE ON DISPLAY: UNDERWATER EXAMPLES FROM SOUTH CAROLINA

James Spirek and Lynn Harris[*]

## 1. INTRODUCTION

Two recently created interpretive paddling and diving trails on the Ashley and Cooper Rivers near Charleston, South Carolina, allow both the diver and non-diver access to remnants of the state's riverine and coastal maritime heritage. Located in South Carolina's Lowcountry, the trails meander through swamps and marshlands inhabited by an array of wildlife including ospreys, bald eagles, ducks, alligators, and fish, especially large catfish. Archaeological sites on the trails include the remains of sailing ships, steamboats, and ferry and plantation landings. These sites are situated in a culturally modified landscape altered from a prehistoric environment of hardwood swamps to one conducive to colonial rice agriculture, and to modern water-control devices including a dam. These sites range in age from the early English colonial period to the beginning of the twentieth century. The purpose of each trail is to communicate to the visitor the historical and archaeological significance of these vestiges of the state's maritime heritage and surrounding maritime cultural landscape. In a more utilitarian sense, the trails also are intended to help stimulate historical tourism to the area.

Initiated by and under the direction of the Underwater Archaeology Division of the South Carolina Institute of Archaeology and Anthropology (SCIAA) at the University of South Carolina, the construction of each trail relied heavily on volunteers, local businesses, and other governmental agencies. Inspired by the successful practice of improving public access to

---

[*] James Spirek and Lynn Harris, South Carolina Institute of Archaeology and Anthropology, University of South Carolina, 1321 Pendleton Street, Columbia, South Carolina 29208.

submerged cultural resources by other state and international programs such as in Florida, New York, Israel, and Australia, SCIAA hoped to embark upon a similar recreational and educational use for a selected few of the state's many intertidal and submerged archaeological assets. In South Carolina there is no specific legislative mandate for SCIAA to improve public access to submerged cultural resources in the state. However, SCIAA interpreted sections of the South Carolina Underwater Antiquities Act of 1991 that are concerned with education as a mandate to improve public access to these underwater museums for educational purposes (S.C.C.L. 54-7-840). Ancillary benefits from this approach also permit SCIAA to promote stewardship, recreation, and tourism centered on selected and monitored cultural resources.

These two trails represent SCIAA's first forays into improving public access to interpreted intertidal and underwater archaeological resources in the state. An earlier proposal by SCIAA in the late 1980s to create an underwater preserve on the remains of the SS *Lawrence*, an iron-hulled steamer that wrecked off Port Royal Sound in 1899, never went beyond the early planning stages. Local divers and dive shop owners showed no enthusiasm for the project, mainly objecting to the winds and currents that made the site a fickle place to dive (Beard, 1990). Subsequently, the idea to create this and other preserves was abandoned. Several years later the notion to provide interpreted public access to the state's maritime resources was revived under the direction of Lynn Harris, SCIAA's manager of the Sport Diving Archaeological Management Program. Harris combined her professional interest in shipwrecks and her recreational pursuits of canoeing and kayaking to create the Ashley River Trail.

## 2. ASHLEY RIVER TRAIL

In 1995, a SCIAA Research Affiliate, Billy Judd, located thirteen intertidal watercraft sites along a four mile stretch of the Ashley River. The watercraft remains represented a diverse range of wooden sailing and motorized vessels, a barge, and a tugboat of composite wood and concrete construction, all from the eighteenth to twentieth centuries, although the majority of the vessels date from the nineteenth century. Those sites were later recorded by SCIAA personnel and volunteers using funds awarded from the Robert L. Stephenson Archaeological Research Fund, a SCIAA in-house grant program (Figure 1). Two of the motorized vessels had copious amounts of phosphate nuggets inside the hulls that suggested an affiliation with the phosphate industry which flourished in South Carolina from 1867 to the demise of the industry at the turn of the last century (Harris, 1995; Harris, 1996).

Concurrently, a state-wide heritage tourism initiative--the South Carolina Heritage Corridor--commenced under the direction of the South Carolina

# MARITIME HERITAGE ON DISPLAY

**Figure 1.** Recording remains of an intertidal wreck at low tide on the Ashley River Trail (SCIAA photograph).

Department of Parks, Recreation, and Tourism (SCPRT). Envisioned to run from the Upcountry to the Lowcountry, or for non-South Carolinians, from the mountains to the coast, the SCPRT planned the corridor for visitors to undertake independent exploration of a series of trails along forests, bays, canals, and rivers by means of walking, canoeing, kayaking, and biking. The SCPRT solicited trail nominations, and SCIAA in turn asked for sport diver input regarding the addition of an underwater component to the corridor. SCIAA suggested a set of criteria including accessibility, popularity, safety, historic theme, and photographic potential for the divers to keep in mind when proposing a site. Responses received from sport divers were mixed; some inappropriately wanted sites where they could collect artifacts or fossils, or nominated shipwrecks located outside of state waters, but local divers generally were positive and enthusiastic about the concept (Harris, 1995b).

SCPRT invited Harris to participate in the corridor development as a member of the Area IV board representing Charleston, Colleton, and

Dorchester counties. The board wanted to portray neglected aspects of South Carolina history and Harris suggested a trail accessible by canoers or kayakers focused on maritime heritage. Fortuitously, the recently documented wrecks proved ideally suited for just such a trail. Heartily endorsed by the regional corridor committee, the paddling trail provided an opportunity to incorporate the rivers and watercraft remains as a theme in the overall scope of the heritage corridor. The theme of the trail encompassed the vital economic connection with Charleston, plantation history, and local industries such as phosphate mining, transportation, and technology that formed an important part of the local story but had not yet been fully explored.

Most of the wreck sites on the Ashley River Trail are visible only at low tide. With a tidal range of as much as four feet, paddling to view the ten wrecks must revolve around the tides. Equipped with a laminated slate developed by SCIAA, a paddler relies on the illustrated guide to navigate through the trail. The slates also offer historical and archaeological information discussing the demise of the vessels, their use on the river, phosphate mining, vernacular shipbuilding, and adjacent historic properties such as Magnolia Plantation and Middleton Place. Alternately, paddlers can arrange guided tours through Old Dorchester State Historical Park or Middleton Place Plantation; trail slates are available from both of these locations. On these guided tours, visitors also can stroll about these two historic sites--Dorchester is an archaeological park centered on the remains of an abandoned colonial town active from 1695 to the 1750s and Middleton Place was an eighteenth- and nineteenth-century rice plantation and is now a tourist attraction. Accompanied by a visit to the park or plantation, the trail visitor can link the history of the adjacent lands with that of the waterway. To quote Park Officer and Ranger Ty Houck, the primary park guide for the paddling trail:

> It is a unique paddle trip because it is literally a flowing timeline. It is a one-of-a-kind program where you can paddle in an idyllic natural setting without leaving the suburbs and see shipwrecks without getting wet. At the upper reaches of the trail it is wild and scenic with blue herons flying overhead, and alligators sunning on the banks amongst the spider lilies. As we get closer to the park, colonial shipwrecks and phosphate mining barges begin to appear, followed by the subdivision of Ashborough gently bringing us into the modern day.

The park organizes approximately twelve tours a year that range from four to sixteen people, and who vary in age from teens to septuagenarians. The History Club of the Citadel has visited the trail at least three times. Word about the trail is communicated through the Park's Internet site and *Park View* publication, flyers, word of mouth, and outside media sources, primarily newspapers. Many of the paddlers respond with positive comments about the trail and appreciate the ability to view shipwrecks and nature at the same time.

The only downside is that the park has a limited number of canoes and demand for paddling the trail is exceeding supply. The park rangers hope to obtain a small grant to purchase more canoes in the near future. On the upside, the trail requires virtually no maintenance, and the guides monitor the sites for any signs of deterioration. In one example of site maintenance, SCIAA reattached a vessel's keelson to the frames with stainless steel fasteners to prevent the timber from washing away.

## 3. COOPER RIVER UNDERWATER HERITAGE TRAIL

In discussing ways to improve public access to archaeological sites for divers, SCIAA considered the merits of creating a preserve centered on an individual site or to link a group of sites into a trail. Ultimately, the trail idea proved more attractive for a number of archaeological and logistical reasons. Most notably, there existed a cohesive group of suitable wrecks easily accessible on the west branch of the Cooper River and the SCIAA field office in Charleston was conveniently close to the sites for implementing field operations and for monitoring the trail in the future. In 1997, the Division received a $7,500 grant from the United States Department of Transportation's Federal Highway Administration's National Recreational Trails Program which was administered by the SCPRT to develop a trail for scuba divers. Matching funds were secured through the use of donated time by volunteer sport divers. Berkeley County public works, a private construction firm, and two local dive shops provided in-kind support for trail construction. Additionally, a private individual donated $500 for use on the trail. Later, Harris obtained two SCIAA Archaeological Research Trust grants totaling $3,700 to more fully record two of the wreck sites.

SCIAA's plans for the trail included introducing mooring buoys to prevent anchor damage to the wrecks, and also creating slates depicting each site and providing diving advice aimed towards minimizing inadvertent damage to the wrecks. In the fall of 1997, SCIAA organized a meeting and invited historic preservationists, fellow archaeologists, sport divers, and dive shop owners to discuss creating the trail. Unexpectedly, response from the sport diving community was ambivalent. Instead of endorsing an opportunity to improve public access for diving as was expected, the divers and dive shop owners in attendance stated their belief that more divers on these sites would adversely impact the wreck sites. SCIAA countered that these sites had already suffered extensive damage by having been completely stripped of artifacts during the 1970s by sport divers. Additionally, these sites already had high visitation from sport divers through individual visits and dive shop sponsored tours. In fact, this stretch of the river is one of the most frequented dive spots in South Carolina. SCIAA's management position contended that, by enhancing public access to these sites, chances for their long-term preservation were improved by lessening harmful impacts made by anchors and divers. At a subsequent meeting, and with time to reflect on the proposal and the resulting benefits, the divers and dive shop owners proved more amenable to launching and assisting the project.

Over a period of several months in 1998, SCIAA worked in conjunction with volunteers to record the remains of six trail sites ranging in age from the early 1700s to the early 1900s. Historical and archaeological data about the sites also were gathered. Fortunately, a copious amount of information existed from previous SCIAA work in the area and from the efforts of the Cooper River Survey Project, a survey team composed of a group of sport divers working under the guidance of SCIAA to document the archaeological remains along this stretch of the river (Harris et al., 1993). Additionally, the Division received two SCIAA Archaeological Research Trust grants in 1999 and 2000 to conduct more in-depth investigation of two wrecks on the trail, the Pimlico and Mepkin Abbey Wrecks.

Conceivably, and depending on the tides and other variables such as time to wander about viewing the sites, a diver to the Cooper River Heritage Trail, which is touted as a blackwater diving experience, could complete the whole circuit of six sites in one visit. If a diver does not finish the trail, they can always come back to complete the tour. The first site on the trail, the Strawberry Wreck, possibly represents the remains of a small British warship burned by Colonel Wade Hampton and his group of partisans during the Revolutionary War. Divers in the past reported finding sheathing with the British broad arrow mark on the wreck. The wreck is in the vicinity of the Strawberry Ferry landing, a cribwork structure constructed of logs, ballast stones, and bricks. The ferry landing was built in 1705 to provide service between Charleston and the frontier town of Childesbury, located on the opposite bank, and outlying settlements (Figure 2).

Heading upstream the diver next visits the Pimlico Wreck, which consists of the remains of a large sailing ship buried in the sand on the edge of the river channel, probably dating to the early to mid-nineteenth century. Recent archaeological investigations revealed a substantial amount of the lower hull of the vessel from bow to stern. Apparently, the ship was stripped and abandoned based on the absence of ballast stones and associated artifacts, although the site is littered with aboriginal ceramic ware, most likely eroded from nearby Native American sites and subsequently deposited in the wreck. The amount of exposed structure varies as sand sweeps back and forth across the wreck depending on tides and the increased flow of released water from the upstream dam.

Continuing onwards the diver next splashes over to inspect the Pimlico barge, which apparently was a towing barge as evidenced by rings on either end that suggest the vessel was towed in train. The barge most likely dates to the late nineteenth to early twentieth century. Completely intact, divers liken the dive experience on the barge to "diving in a bath tub." Towards the marsh

Figure 2. Remains of Strawberry Ferry landing cribwork (SCIAA photograph).

bank, the diver and boat passengers can view the remnants of rice agricultural relics including puncheons to support the dikes and a rice trunk that regulated the flow of water in and out of the rice fields.

The last two sites on the trail, a shipwreck and a landing, are adjacent to an historic plantation associated with Henry Laurens, a prominent colonial planter, merchant, shipowner, and politician. The property was owned by the Laurens family until 1827. Divers located the wreck in the mid-1970s and found cargo consisting of siding planks and a multitude of stoneware jugs that dated the wreck to the early 1800s. The remains of the small sailing vessel, which show evidence of burning, consist of the lower hull, extant from bow to the mortise of the stern post. The stern post and rudder were recovered by SCIAA in 1980 for analysis and indicated the vessel was constructed of local woods. Lines recorded from the vessel, probably a work boat, show it to be flat-bottomed with a hard chine at the turn of the bilge (Wilbanks, 1981). The Mepkin landing, a log and ballast stone crib work, was constructed using mortise and tenon joinery and was used to load and offload goods and products destined for plantation use or sale in Charleston. Scattered about the landing are artifacts including bricks, tiles, ceramics, and miscellaneous iron fasteners. The property currently is owned by Trappist monks who run the Mepkin Abbey.

## 4. TRAIL INTERPRETATION AND MANAGEMENT

Infrastructure to support the trail includes a brochure, laminated slates, mooring buoys, and guidelines. The brochure provides a brief promotional synopsis of the trail for potential visitors. Six interpretive slates are available at local dive shops. An introductory slate provides a history of the river's usage, local flora and fauna, mooring details, and diving information, especially in regards to blackwater diving; a trail map is located on the reverse side. The remaining five slates focus on a particular site or group of sites. Each slate consists of a site plan and a discussion of the historical usage or theme associated with the site, such as rice agriculture, local economy, riverine and coastal watercraft, shipbuilding, and any special diving instructions. The moorings consist of a buoy and a three hundred and forty-pound cement block staked into the marl river bottom. The blocks serve to anchor boats and to provide a pedestal for signage. Guidelines radiate out from the mooring blocks to the archaeological site. The guidelines are necessary as visibility in the river is highly variable, depending on tide and season. Maintenance of the trail focuses primarily on monitoring the six buoys and hardware, which may become fouled from floating vegetation and accidental boat strikes, among other minor "nuts and bolts" issues. Originally conceived as a year-round trail, maintenance issues cause the trail to be closed from October to April. This affords the opportunity to clean buoys, restore mooring apparatus, and fix any other problems.

Since the completion of the main trail work in the spring of 1999, several enhancements or changes to the trail have transpired. An unexpected enhancement of the trail occurred in the fall of 1999 with the addition of a large ship anchor which had been illegally retrieved from within the trail area by local divers. Under SCIAA supervision, the anchor was placed at the Pimlico barge site, although not its original location, due to the relative ease of returning the nine hundred-pound anchor to the river with a crane at this site. Another anchor, snagged by a shrimper in the southeastern part of the state, was added to the trail in 2000. With no funds to conserve the anchor the decision was made to place it next to the first anchor and to monitor its condition. In the fall of 2000, the stern post and rudder were returned to the Mepkin Wreck (Figure 3). The timbers were staked near the stern of the vessel after reconstituting the assembly with synthetic rods. Addition of this assembly now affords the diver a more complete picture of the construction of a colonial ship.

In addition to focusing on individual trail sites, the interpretive materials also discuss the surrounding environment. Essentially, the whole river system

**Figure 3.** Divers resting before replacing the Mepkin Wreck rudder and stern post (SCIAA photograph).

bears signs of human intervention: the immediate landscape was altered from cypress swamps to rice fields through slave labor; the Lake Moultrie Dam, upriver of the trail, regulates the flow of the river; Old Santee Canal, built to improve navigation to the interior, and Durham Cut, used to access the trail, were dug in the early 1900s to divert freshwater to Charleston. The printed materials also point out other nearby cultural attractions, including plantations, Old Santee Canal State Park, Mepkin Abbey, and Cypress Gardens, that divers and their families might like to visit during their stay in the area.

Visitation at the trail is mostly channeled through the three local dive shops in the Greater Charleston area. Most use the sites as a training ground for easing divers into a blackwater experience. SCIAA also employs the sites on the trail during a Field Training Course for sport divers to teach them the basics of recording shipwrecks. Individual divers also visit the trail. SCIAA still is working on developing ways to gather feedback from visitors and to respond to their concerns or problems about the trail. The trail program still is evolving and SCIAA envisions it continuing to develop over the years with the possible inclusion of other sites, as well as through augmenting interpretation of existing sites with new information. A trail webpage also is in development, both for the non-diving public and for those who would like to plan a trip to the trail.

## 5. CONCLUSION

The Ashley and Cooper River Trails provide opportunities for visiting divers and paddlers to easily access and explore intertidal and submerged remnants of South Carolina's maritime heritage. These forays into providing public access to submerged cultural resources have proved beneficial by promoting the historical and archaeological significance of these selected sites to a range of organizations and individuals who otherwise might not have joined forces to protect their maritime heritage. At the present time, SCIAA is attending to the Cooper River Trail with buoy maintenance and continued documentation. No immediate plans exist to create another trail or preserve in the state; however, additional sites may be developed for public visitation. In the meantime, the trails are open to all to enjoy the maritime heritage of South Carolina in an open air and underwater museum.

## REFERENCES

Beard, D. V., 1990, The SS *William Lawrence*: South Carolina's first archaeological preserve?, *The Goody Bag*, 1(2):5-6, Newsletter of the Underwater Archaeology Division, South Carolina Institute of Archaeology and Anthropology, University of South Carolina, Columbia.

Harris, L., 1996, Shipwreck work continues on banks of the Ashley River, *Flotsam and Jetsam*, 7(1):4-5, Newsletter of the Underwater Archaeology Division, South Carolina Institute of Archaeology and Anthropology, University of South Carolina, Columbia.

Harris, L., 1995, Wreck graveyard found in the Ashley River, *Flotsam and Jetsam*, 6(2):1&3, Newsletter of the Underwater Archaeology Division, South Carolina Institute of Archaeology and Anthropology, University of South Carolina, Columbia.

Harris, L., 1995b, Dive sites to be included in the South Carolina Heritage Corridor, *Flotsam and Jetsam*, 6(2):4, Newsletter of the Underwater Archaeology Division, South Carolina Institute of Archaeology and Anthropology, University of South Carolina, Columbia.

Harris, L., Moss, J., and Naylor, C., 1993, *The Cooper River Survey: An Underwater Reconnaissance of the West Branch*, Research Manuscript Series 218, South Carolina Institute of Archaeology and Anthropology, University of South Carolina, Columbia.

Wilbanks, R., 1981, A preliminary report on the Mepkin Abbey Wreck, Cooper River, South Carolina: An early 19th Century river trading vessel, in: *Underwater Archaeology: The Challenge Before Us, the Proceedings of the Twelfth Conference on Underwater Archaeology*, G. P. Watts Jr., ed., Fathom Eight, New Orleans, pp. 151-158.

# CONCLUSION

The intent of this book was to bring together in one volume as much as possible of the available thought and practice regarding underwater archaeological preserves, parks, and trails. The main goal of this submerged cultural resource management concept is relatively straightforward: to create opportunities for public access to interpreted shipwrecks. Themes of education, recreation, and historic preservation are central to this concept. Concrete examples provided here of the legislation, presentation, and implementation of this concept demonstrate the varied means of achieving the desired result world-wide by allowing divers and non-divers access to submerged cultural remains otherwise obscured by water and sediment and the fog of time.

Shipwrecks, and other submerged cultural resources, throughout the world are subject to increasing pressure exerted by those intent on possessing a piece of history. Often it seems as if the only useful shipwreck or artifact is the one on display in a museum or on the mantelpiece. The chapters in this volume attest to another precept, that the best place for a shipwreck is underwater, embedded in its grave. Visitors to a shipwreck can witness the ruin of human industry as they float, drift, and glide through innerspace. All the senses are called upon to experience a fish-inhabited, barnacle-encrusted, sand-entombed shipwreck. Observing the steady process of devolving construct to evolving reef is as much a learning experience as seeing a shipwreck in a museum or an artifact in a display case.

The shipwreck encounter can be enhanced in many ways by the submerged cultural resource manager. Creating access to a shipwreck is the main goal once the decision is made to establish an underwater preserve, park, or trail. Many forms of access are viable, including providing mooring buoys, publishing informative brochures and underwater slates, creating land-based exhibits, posting websites, and enhancing a site through repatriation of actual components or placement of artifact replicas, to name a few. Perhaps the most important method of access is the content of interpretive materials that convey to the visitor the historical and archaeological significance of an underwater archaeological site and its surrounding environment. Hopefully, by opening a hatch to the past for visitors, the submerged cultural resource manager can instill the concept of preservation in place, and can begin to foster a sense of stewardship, ensuring sustainability of the resource for future divers and non-divers to visit, explore, and learn.

The editors and authors intend for this volume to serve as a primer for those interested in promoting public access to interpreted shipwrecks and other submerged cultural sites. Through the efforts and experiences recorded in this book, we hope others may find guidance and inspiration as they develop underwater archaeological preserves, parks, and trails in their region.

Although practiced in relatively few areas of the world at this writing, the concept is a sound one, provided the reason for and manner of creating access is in the best interest of the resource. We hope this book will help to expand the establishment of underwater archaeological preserves, parks, and trails throughout the world and will continue to promote the vital message of preserving these resources as irreplaceable pieces of our sunken maritime past.

# APPENDIX A

The following is a list of the participants and paper titles in the SHA 2000 symposium that was the basis for this work. For a number of reasons not all of the participants were able to contribute to the book:

James D. Spirek and Della A. Scott-Ireton "Introduction to Session."

Shane Guest "Description or Interpretation: Public Access to the Underwater Heritage of Australia."

Todd Hannahs "Preservation, Communication or Recreation: Underwater Historic Parks or Preserves."

Kenneth J. Vrana and Gail A. Vander Stoep "The Maritime Landscape of the Thunder Bay Underwater Preserve."

John R. Halsey and Peter Lindquist "Beneath Pictured Rocks."

Joseph W. Zarzynski "Colonial Warships and an Underwater Classroom: Submerged Heritage in a Mountain Lake."

Arthur B. Cohn "Lake Champlain's Underwater Historic Preserve Program."

Susan B.M. Langley "Historic Shipwreck Preserves in Maryland."

Della A. Scott-Ireton "Preservation, Protection, Promotion: Florida's Underwater Archaeological Preserve System."

Jefferson J. Gray "Diving in the Dairyland: Developing Wisconsin's Maritime Trails."

James D. Spirek and Lynn B. Harris "Maritime Heritage on Display: Underwater Examples from South Carolina."

Bruce G. Terrell "Florida Keys National Marine Shipwreck Sanctuary Trail: A Model for Multiple-Use Resource Management."

Jim Adams "Biscayne National Park: A Case Study in Maritime Cultural Resource Management."

Tim J. Smith "Maritime Heritage 'Down Under': Twenty-five Years of Reaching the Public *An Australian Success Story?"

Daniel La Roche "Cultural Resource Management and the Presentation of Canadian Submerged Heritage: A Review of Past Experience and Thoughts on the Future."

Roger C. Smith, Discussant

# INDEX

A.R. Noyes, 86, 88
Abandoned Shipwreck Act, 48, 65, 66, 86, 154, 155
*Adelaide Baker*, 159, 160
*Alert*, 61
Alexander's Wreck: *see Amesbury*
*Alligator*, 154
America (*see also* United States), 7, 22, 32, 61, 109, 151, 154
*Amesbury*, 161
Antilles, Lesser, 61
Archaeological Resources Protection Act, 48
Atlantic Ocean, 57, 69, 161
Australia, v, 119, 121-124, 128, 130, 131, 1135-139, 142-147, 166
Avocational, 1, 5, 30, 39, 104, 134

Bahamas, 153
*Ballista*, 79
*Benwood*, 158
Bermuda, 112, 113, 116
British Columbia, 39
Burlington Bay Horse Ferry, 87, 88

Canada, 3, 29-34, 36-40
*Capricieux*, 34
Caribbean, 153, 158
*Célèbre*, 32-34, 36
*Champlain II*, 88, 89
Chesapeake Bay, 43, 55

*City of Hawkinsville*, 97, 100
*City of Launceston*, 141
*City of Washington*, 158
Civil War (American), 45, 54, 55, 61, 103, 154
*Clan Ranald*, 145, 146
Commonwealth Historic Shipwrecks Act (Australia), 124
Conservation, 5, 11, 13, 19, 31, 48, 69, 72, 86, 93, 123, 124, 128, 129, 144
*Constellation*, 14
*Constitution*, 14
*Copenhagen*, 97, 100, 101
Cuba, 59, 153, 158
  Havana, 158
Cultural tourism (*see also* heritage tourism), 135, 146

*Dartmouth*, 71, 72, 74-76, 79, 81, 82
Diamond Island Stone Boat, 88
*Divemaster*, 115, 116
*Duane*, 158, 159

*Eagle*, 158
Ecosystem, 27, 36
England, 31, 72, 73, 75, 98
*Entreprenant*, 34
Europe, 22, 24, 35, 135, 153

*F. Carver*: see Adelaide Baker
Florida, v-vii, 43, 65-67, 95-105, 119, 151-156, 158, 160, 162, 166
  Apalachicola, 97
  Boynton Beach, 104
  Bradenton Beach, 104
  Florida State University, 96
  Ft. Pierce, 96
  Islamorada, v, 97
  Keys, v, 96, 119, 151-155, 157-159, 162
  Key Biscayne, 98
  Key Largo, 157
  Key West, 152, 153, 157, 161
  Marathon, 157, 159, 160
  Miami, 98
  Old Town, 97
  Panama City, 97
  Pensacola, 97, 100
  Pompano Beach, 97
  St. Augustine, 104
  Suwannee River, 97
  University of Miami, 98
Florida Department of Environmental Protection, 156
Florida Department of State, 96
Florida Division of Historical Resources, 95
France, 31, 158

*General Butler*, 86
*Germania*: see *Half Moon*
Germany, 45, 97, 98
Great Britain, 43, 80
Great Lakes, 17, 21, 22, 24, 37, 107, 109-112, 114, 116, 117, 151
  Erie, 109
  Huron, 22, 109, 110
  Michigan, 21, 109, 114
  Ontario, 109
  Superior, 21, 22, 44, 107-109, 111-114
*Griffon*, 109

Gulf of Mexico, 97, 153, 158

*Half Moon*, 98
*Hazardous*, 75
Heritage South Australia, 139
Heritage tourism (see also cultural tourism), 7, 49, 53, 101, 122, 166
Heritage Victoria, 141
Historic preservation, vi-viii, 1, 3, 7-11, 13-15, 21, 23, 40, 48, 86, 88, 90, 101, 154, 156, 157, 169
Historic Scotland, 72-74, 79
*Huron*, 59-69

*Ida S. Dow*, 52
Indiana University, 96, 154
*Iona II*, 75
Ireland, 80
Israel. viii, 166

Lawrence, 166
*Le Prudent*, 34
Legislation, viii, 1, 29, 36, 39, 40, 43, 48, 65, 72, 110, 119, 122
*Lofthus*, 104
*Lorain*: see Steven M. Selvick
Louisiana
  New Orleans, 97, 153

*Machault*, 30
Maine
  Bangor, 159
*Maine*, 158
Maritime Archaeological and Historical Society, 48
Maryland, 43, 45, 46, 48-50, 52-57
  Douglas Point, 54
  Historic St Mary's City, 55, 56
  Mallows Bay, 45, 52-56

# INDEX

Point Lookout, 45, 55
*Maryland Dove*, 56
Maryland Historical Trust, 48, 49, 52, 57
*Massachusetts* (BB-2), 97, 100, 101
Media, 12, 52, 75, 99, 110, 123, 130, 144, 167
*Menemon Sanford*, 154
Mepkin Abbey Wreck, 170, 172, 173
Merchant Shipping Act (UK), 72
*Mesquite*, 113
*Metropolis*, 61
Mexico, 61
Michigan, 3, 21-23, 44, 107, 109-113, 154
  Alpena, 18
  Munising, 111, 114-117
Michigan Department of Natural Resources, 112
Michigan Public Act 452, 109, 112
Michigan Public Law 184, 107, 109
Middle East, 135
*Miss Munising*, 116
Museum, 18, 24, 27, 30, 32, 49, 50, 52-55, 69, 72, 85, 88, 91, 92, 98, 99, 101, 117, 119, 121-123, 128, 135-139, 142, 144, 146, 166, 174

National Marine Sanctuary Act, 151
National Oceanic and Atmospheric Administration (NOAA), 22, 151, 152, 154-157
National Park Service (NPS), 18, 19, 21, 57, 112
National Register of Historic Places, v, 7, 21, 63, 99
National Trust of Australia, 129
Native American, 22, 24, 54, 104, 170
Natural resources, 17, 18, 21, 54, 151, 157
Nature Conservancy, 54, 156
Nautical Archaeology Society (NAS), 34, 74
*New Orleans*, 25, 26
New South Wales, 124-126, 128, 131, 132, 136, 142, 143
  Maroubra Beach, 143
  Newcastle, 142
  Sydney, 128
New South Wales Heritage Office, 126, 131
New South Wales National Parks & Wildlife Service, 128
New York, 88, 92, 93, 154, 158, 166
  Lake George, 154
North America, 32, 87, 88, 109
*North America*, 161
North Atlantic Squadron, 61
North Carolina, 43, 46, 61, 64-66, 68
  Cape Hatteras, 59
  East Carolina University, 64
  Nags Head, 59-62, 65, 67, 68
  Outer Banks, 62, 68
North Carolina Department of Cultural Resources, 63, 65-67
North Carolina Historical Commission, 66
Northern Ireland, 73
Northern Territory (Australia), 136, 137
  Arnhem Land, 136
Nova Scotia, 31
  Louisbourg Harbor, 31, 35, 36

*O.J. Walker*, 90, 91
Ohio
  Cleveland, 114
Ontario, 30, 36, 39, 40, 110

*P.S. Manning*, 129
Parks Canada, 29-34, 35-40
Pennsylvania, 61
  Chester, 59, 158
*Phoenix*, 86

Pimlico Wreck, 170, 172
Potomac River, 45, 46, 49, 50, 52-55
Protection of Wrecks Act (UK), 72-75, 79

Québec, vii, 39
  Québec City, vii
Queensland, 124, 136, 137
  Great Barrier Reef, 124
  James Cook University, 136
  Magnetic Island, 136

*Randolph*: see *Thunderbolt*
*Ranger*, 61
Red Bay *chalupa*, 30, 31
Red Bay whaler, 30
*Regina*, 104
*Resurgam*, 75
Revolutionary War (American), 52, 57, 170
Royal Navy (British), 79

Salvage, v, 5, 24, 30, 33, 46, 52, 62, 65, 96, 104, 109, 153, 158, 161
Salvor, 5, 153, 155, 159
*San Pedro*, v, 66, 97, 99, 104, 158, 159
Scotland, viii, 71-74, 80
  Duart Point, 74
  Oban, 75
  Sound of Mull, 71-76, 79, 80
  University of St Andrews, 74
Scotland Act (UK), 73
*Seaprobe Atlantis*, 71
Signage, 14, 86 123, 127, 128, 130, 132, 144, 146, 172
*Smith Moore*, 111
South America, 61
South Australia, 124, 136, 137, 139-142, 146
  Coorong, 142

  Garden Island, 139
  Kangaroo Island, 139
  Port Adelaide, 139
  Port MacDonnell, 139
  Wardang Island, 139
  York Peninsula, 139, 146
South Carolina, 165, 166, 168, 169, 174
  Charleston, 165, 167-171, 173
  Childesbury, 170
  Magnolia Plantation, 168
  Middleton Place, 168
  Port Royal Sound, 166
  University of South Carolina, 165
South Carolina Department of Parks, Recreation, and Tourism, 168
South Carolina Institute of Archaeology and Anthropology (SCIAA), 165-174
South Carolina Underwater Antiquities Act, 166
Spanish-American War, 97, 158
*Sport*, 107
Sport diver/diving, 43, 46, 48, 65, 74, 79, 85, 96, 98, 99, 102, 103, 109, 110, 114, 117, 119, 153, 167, 169, 170, 173
Steven M. Selvick, 113, 114
Strawberry Wreck, 170, 171
*Swan*, 71, 72, 74-79
*Sweepstake*, 37, 38

*Tarpon*, 97, 101
Tasmania, 124, 136, 137
  Bruny Island, 136
  King Island, 136
Texas
  Galveston, 153
  Texas A&M University, 88
*Thunderbolt*, 160
Treasure hunter/hunting, 13, 96, 104, 153, 160

# INDEX

U-352, 46
U-1105, 47-51
United Kingdom (UK), 71-73, 75, 83
  Channel Islands, 73
  Isle of Man, 73
  Orkney, 71
  Skye, 72
United Kingdom Department for Culture, Media and Sport, 72
United States (US) (*see also* America), vii, viii, 18, 21, 46, 61, 98, 109, 112, 119, 153
United States Army, 61, 68, 160
United States Bureau of Land Management, 54
United States Coast Guard, 48, 50, 86, 116, 158
United States Congress, 61, 64, 69
United States Department of Transportation, 54, 169
United States Lifesaving Service, 61, 69
United States Navy, 48, 49, 57, 61, 62, 65, 66, 68, 98, 154
  Historical Center, 49, 66
*Urca de Lima*, 95, 104


Vermont, 43, 65, 66, 86, 91, 92
  Burlington, 86-88
  Lake Champlain, 43, 85-93, 154
  University of Vermont, 88, 91
Vermont Division for Historic Preservation, 86, 88, 90
Vermont Historic Preservation Act, 86
Victoria, 124, 131, 136, 137, 139, 141, 142, 146
  Beware Reef, 141
  Melbourne, 141, 142
  Moonlight Head, 142
  Port Phillip Heads, 141
*Victory*, 14
Virginia, 49, 50

Hampton Roads, 59


Wales, 73
War of 1812, 57
West Virginia
  Point Pleasant, 160
Western Australia, 121-124, 136-139, 141
  Albany, 138
  Exmouth, 138
  Perth, 122
  Rottnest Island, 122, 123, 135, 137
*William Salthouse*, 145
Wisconsin
  Sturgeon Bay, 114
World War I, 45, 52, 53, 97
World War II, 43, 45, 52, 154, 158